CASS LIBRARY OF AFRICAN STUDIES

MISSIONARY RESEARCHES AND TRAVELS
No. 15

General Editor: ROBERT I. ROTBERG
Associate Professor, Department of Political Science,
Massachusetts Institute of Technology

JOURNAL OF AN EXPEDITION
UP THE
NIGER AND TSHADDA RIVERS

MISSIONARY RESEARCHES AND TRAVELS

No. 10. Frederick Stanley Arnot
Garenganze, Or, Seven Years' Pioneer Mission Work in Central Africa (c. 1886)
With a new introduction by Professor Robert I. Rotberg.
New Edition.

No. 11. Hope Masterman Wadell
Twenty-Nine Years in the West Indies and Central Africa. A Review of Missionary Work and Adventure 1829-1858 (1863)
With a new introduction by G. I. Jones
Second Edition.

No. 12. W. A. Elmslie
Among the Wild Ngoni. (1899)
With a new introductory note by Ian Nance
New Impression.

No. 13. Robert Pickering Ashe
Two Kings of Uganda. Or, Life by the shores of Victoria Nyanza. Being an account of a residence of Six Years in Eastern Equatorial Africa (1889)
With a new introduction by Professor John Rowe.
Second Edition.

No. 14. A. M. Mackay
A. M. Mackay, Pioneer Missionary of the Church Missionary Society to Uganda (1890) by his sister (J. W. H.).
With a new introductory note by Professor D. A. Low.
New Impression.

No. 15. Samuel Crowther
Journal of an Expedition up the Niger and Tshadda Rivers undertaken by Macgregor Laird, Esq., in connection with the British Government in 1854 (1855)
With a new introduction by Professor J. F. A. Ajayi.
Second Edition.

No. 16. Charles New
Life, Wanderings and Labours in Eastern Africa. With an account of the First Successful Ascent of the Equatorial Snow Mountain, Kilima Njaro. And remarks upon East African Slavery (1873, 1874).
With a new introduction by Alison Smith.
Third Edition.

No. 17. Ruth H. Fisher
Twilight Tales of the Black Baganda (1911).
With a new introduction by Professor. Merrick Posnansky.
Second Edition.

No. 18. James Frederick Schön and Samuel Crowther
Journals of the Rev. James Frederick Schön and Mr. Samuel Crowther, who, with her Majesty's Government, accompanied the Expedition of the Niger in 1841, on behalf of the Church Missionary Society (1842).
With a new introduction by Professor J. F. A. Ajayi.
Second Edition.

JOURNAL OF AN EXPEDITION

UP THE

NIGER AND TSHADDA RIVERS

Undertaken by Macgregor Laird in connection with the
British Government in 1854

BY

THE REV. SAMUEL CROWTHER

SECOND EDITION

WITH A NEW INTRODUCTION BY

PROFESSOR J. F. ADE AJAYI

Department of History, University of Ibadan

FRANK CASS & CO. LTD.

1970

Published by
FRANK CASS AND COMPANY LIMITED
67 Great Russell Street, London WC1B 3BT

New introduction Copyright © 1970 J. F. Ade Ajayi

First edition   1855
Second edition   1970

ISBN 0 7146 1866 7

Printed in Great Britain by Clarke, Doble & Brendon Ltd.
Plymouth and London

GENERAL EDITOR'S PREFACE

OF the historically significant books by nineteenth-century missionaries to West Africa, few are by Africans and fewer still are as valuable as those by Samuel Crowther. By the time he came to compose the present *Journal*, Crowther, an ex-slave who was to become the Church Missionary Society's first black bishop, had already achieved fame as the result of the publication of his *Journal* of the 1841 Expedition up the Niger River (also reprinted in this series of *Missionary Researches and Travels*), become ordained, travelled and evangelized throughout Yorubaland, and called on Queen Victoria. He was experienced and observant, and in his introduction to the present volume Professor Ajayi suggests that Crowther's *Journal* of the Expedition of 1854, although less well known than that of 1841, is in fact of greater ethnological and historical significance. For long it has been overshadowed by William B. Baikie's readable *Narrative of an Exploring Voyage up the Rivers Kwara and Binue* (London, 1856; reprinted by Frank Cass), but Crowther's own *Journal* provides an additional dimension as well as a further elaboration of his own ideological development. Its renewed availability should therefore be widely welcomed.

Professor Ajayi, who is head of the Department of History at the University of Ibadan, has already discussed Crowther and his work, and the Expedition, in his *Christian Missions in Nigeria, 1841–1891: The Making of a New Elite* (London, 1965), and edited Crowther's autobiographical narrative for Philip Curtin (ed.), *Africa Remembered: Narratives by West Africans from the Era of the Slave Trade* (Madison, 1967). The present introduction supplements his previous work and complements his introduction, in this same series, to a new edition of *Journals of the Rev. James Frederick Schön and Mr. Samuel Crowther* (London, 1842).

R.I.R.

5 March 1969

INTRODUCTION
TO THE
SECOND EDITION

AFTER all the fanfare about and the tragic failure of the 1841 Expedition,[1] the voyage of the *Pleaid* up the Niger and the Benue River[2] in 1854 was planned on a modest scale. Yet the venture succeeded beyond all expectations. Although it did not cover its costs from the trade in which it engaged, trade was a secondary consideration; more important was the report on the commercial potentialities of the Niger-Benue basin.[3] It is also true that the Expedition did not make contact with Dr.

[1] Christopher C. Ifemesia, "The Civilizing Mission of 1841," *Journal of the Historical Society of Nigeria*, II, 3 (1962), 291–310. Also J. F. A. Ajayi, "A New Introduction" to J. F. Schön and S. A. Crowther, *Journal of the Expedition up the Niger in 1841* (London 1855, reprinted Frank Cass, 1970).

[2] European writers first referred to the Benue as the Tshadda, thinking that it was connected with Lake Chad. This name was unknown to the people at the confluence who distinguished the Niger and Benue as White River and Black River (W. B. Baikie, *Narrative of an Exploring Voyage up the Rivers Kwora and Binue commonly known as the Niger and Tshadda* [London, 1856, reprinted Frank Cass 1966], 73, 426–7). It was Barth who first established its name as Benue ("Binue" or mother of waters in Jukun, and adopted by the Fulani conquerors of Adamawa). *Travels and Discoveries in North and Central Africa 1850–55* (London, 1857–59, reprinted Frank Cass 1965), II, entry for June 18, 1851.

[3] T. J. Hutchinson, *Narrative of the Niger, Tshadda, and Binue Exploration including a report on the position and prospects of trade up those rivers, with remarks on the malaria and fevers of Western Africa* (London, 1855, reprinted Frank Cass 1966), 240–257.

Heinrich Barth at Yola as hoped. But in reaching Muri,[1] so close to Adamawa, the *Pléaid* had penetrated some 250 miles farther upstream than any previous European vessel and had established the fact that a continuous trade route existed across Africa from Tripoli to Bornu and Adamawa, and down the Benue and Niger Rivers to the Atlantic Ocean. Above all, apart from fifty-four Africans, twelve Europeans spent sixteen weeks on the voyage and, by regularly taking quinine, they avoided any serious illness or death. This was a spectacular achievement which opened the way for a rapid expansion of European activities not only in the Niger basin, but in Africa as a whole. However, this significant event was overshadowed at the time by the Crimean War, which prevented an immediate follow up, and Laird's voyage has not always received the attention it deserves in the history of European relations with Africa.

Similarly, while Crowther's *Journal* of the 1841 Expedition achieved immediate fame, his 1854 *Journal* is little known or appreciated. The reputation of the earlier *Journal* has been enhanced not only by the publicity given to the 1841 Expedition but also by the inclusion in it of the fascinating story of his early life and enslavement. His 1854 *Journal* has also been overshadowed by the excellent official report issued by Dr. William Baikie, who worked closely with Crowther and had the advantage of using Crowther's *Journal*.[2] Yet Baikie's work supplements and does not replace that of Crowther, who had the immense advantage of being able to communicate directly with the people, and who had an appreciation of the human situation and problems

---

[1] Crowther and Baikie called it the Kingdom of Hamaruwa. In fact, Hamaruwa was the name of the first emir and the correct name is the emirate of Muri. The expedition reached the main port at Garuwa. (A. H. M. Kirk-Greene, *Adamawa Past and Present* [London, 1958]).

[2] Baikie, *Narrative of an Exploring Voyage*, 410, formally acknowledged "the pleasure I derived from your [Crowther's] company, and the information I have reaped from you."

which Baikie could not claim. Undoubtedly, too, Crowther's 1854 *Journal* is a far more important work than his 1841 *Journal* because of both the wider area covered and the greater maturity of the author. It is Crowther's most important book apart from his publications on the Yoruba language.

The 1854 Expedition arose out of the continued faith of Macgregor Laird, a Liverpool businessman, in the commercial potential of the lower Niger basin.[1] Following a disastrous failure in 1832, when forty of the forty-nine Europeans on the expedition to the Niger led by him died and he was ruined financially, he watched others, such as Robert Jamieson and John Beecroft, and the British government, attempt with no greater success between 1836 and 1842, to open up the Niger to regular European commercial traffic. He followed with interest the expansion of missionary and commercial activities along the West African coast and through the Bight of Benin into the Yoruba country between 1842 and 1851. He welcomed the consolidation of the British position with the appointment of Beecroft as a Consul in 1849 and the imposition of a pro-British regime at Lagos in December 1851.[2] He then put forward two proposals to the government: (1) a contract for a monthly mail boat to run between Liverpool and Fernando Po calling at all major West African ports and offering passages for the petty businessmen, particularly Sierra Leonean traders and would-be emigrants; (2) a revival of Niger exploration which, if successful, would lead to a similar contract for regular traffic on the Niger and would also encourage the small businessmen and Sierra Leonean settlers and missionaries.

[1] For Macgregor Laird (1808–61), younger son of William Laird, notable ship-building family of Birkenhead, see John E. Flint, *Sir George Goldie and the Making of Nigeria* (London, 1960), 13–21.

[2] Kenneth Onwuka Dike, *Trade and Politics in the Niger Delta* (Oxford, 1956), 128–134; J. F. A. Ajayi, "The British Occupation of Lagos, 1851–61", *Nigeria Magazine*, 69 (August, 1961), 97–106.

The government was cautious. They awarded a contract for the mail boat along the coast,[1] but hesitated about reviving Niger exploration. The mail boats operated by Laird's African Steamship Company were an immediate success in terms of the amount of regular traffic they generated. There was a rapid expansion of the palm-oil trade, and other produce, such as shea-butter, indigo, and, particularly, cotton, was tried out on the market. The mail boats were particularly helpful to the Sierra Leonean traders who could not afford their own vessels and the complement of staff necessary to run them and maintain off-shore establishments. They booked passages on the mail boats and paid freight on their trade goods. Eventually, they began to consider how to break the monopoly established by the European firms.[2] The mail boats were also particularly useful to the different missionaries not only because they profited from the increasing prosperity of the Sierra Leonean traders but also because the alternative source of transportation made them less dependent on the European trading firms. This was very valuable in the period when the missionaries supported the Sierra Leonean traders in their effort to break the monopoly of the European firms.[3]

This increased traffic along the coast and the consolidation of British power at Lagos acted as a powerful stimulus to the expansion of British trade and missionary activities in the interior of the Yoruba country. A direct result was a better acquaintance with the routes going from the Yoruba country to the cities and markets of the Sokoto Caliphate and Bornu, as well as more information about the resources and potential of these markets for

---

[1] *Parliamentary Papers* 1852, XLIX (284) *Correspondence Relating to the Conveyance of H.M. Mails to West Coast Africa.*

[2] For example, see Dike, *Trade and Politics in the Niger Delta,* 119–120.

[3] *Ibid.* The position changed radically toward the end of the century when the misionary societies became more nationalistic and supported European firms against the interest of the small African traders, for example on the Niger: Flint, *Goldie,* 97–98.

increased trade. This activity stimulated interest in these overland routes; and, as was often the case in Nigerian history, it in turn stimulated new interest in the alternative route offered by the Niger-Benue waterway.

It was these increased activities along the coast and in the Yoruba hinterland of Lagos as much as the news of Barth's fantastic journeys in the Sudan and southwards to Adamawa that rekindled government interest in Niger exploration. If the Niger-Benue waterway could be opened up to regular European traffic it would not merely shift the trader's frontier inland from the coast; it would also tap the resources of the powerful and well-organised kingdoms that Barth was visiting. Macgregor Laird was to bear much of the cost of the expedition. The government grant was a modest £5,000 in return for free passage for three government officials whose interests and activities were to take precedence over Laird's commercial involvement.[1] Laird also agreed to offer free passage to Samuel Crowther in furtherance of his belief that the expansion of trade and Christian civilisation on the Niger would be mutually beneficial and that the Sierra Leoneans had an important role to play in both.[2]

By 1854, Crowther was a mature and experienced missionary and traveller of about forty-eight years of age. In addition to his early journeys in the Yoruba country as a slave boy in 1821-2 and his voyage to freedom in Freetown, he first visited Britain in 1826. This visit was followed by his training at Fourah Bay College, his employment as a school teacher in different parts of the colony, and his appointment to the staff of Fourah Bay College in 1834. After his experiences during the 1841 Expedition, he paid a second visit to Britain in 1842 for

---

[1] Hutchinson, *Narrative of the Niger, Tshadda and Binue Exploration*, 9.

[2] "Mr. Laird's Instructions to Mr. T. C. Taylor, Sailing Master of the *Pleaid*", May 8, 1854, para. 7, in Baikie, *Narrative of an Exploring Voyage*, 407.

further training at the Church Missionary Society
Training College at Islington. He was ordained in 1843,
and sent as a missionary to Yorubaland. He worked at
Badagri in 1845–46 and Abeokuta between 1846 and 1854.
During these years he travelled widely in the Yoruba
country and continued his study of the Yoruba language
and institutions. He also visited Britain in 1851, when
he met Queen Victoria and Lord Palmerston, in order to
strengthen the Society's attempt to persuade the British
government forcibly to intervene in Lagos politics.[1]

It was because of this wide experience that he was
asked to join another Niger Expedition in 1854. By then
the Society's mission in the Yoruba country was embarking on a period of rapid expansion.[2] A station at
Ibadan had just been opened and there was considerable
interest in expanding also into the main areas with
which Ibadan had regular commercial and political
connections.[3] Moreover, Hausaland and Bornu continued
to exercise strong attractions as mission fields.[4] This
stimulated the Society's concern with both the land and
the river routes to the north. In other words, the Society
was interested in further Niger explorations in pursuit of
their ambition to gain access to what they referred to
vaguely as "Hausaland."

Apart from these concerns, the Ibo, Igalla, Nupe, and
others among the liberated Africans in Sierra Leone,
irrespective of religious affiliations, were urging the
Society to establish a Niger mission. Such a mission,

---

[1] J. F. A. Ajayi, *Christian Missions in Nigeria, 1841–90:
The Making of a New Elite* (London, 1965), 72–74.

[2] See below, XX. Crowther learnt at the Niger-Benue
confluence that Ibadan soldiers were assisting "Dasaba" (i.e.
Masaba) in an effort to establish his rule in Nupe against the
claims of Usman Zaki. The Balẹ of Ibadan later confirmed that
there were about a thousand Ibadan soldiers involved. Crowther's
argument was that the line of missionary expansion should follow
the political alignments indicated by the Ibadan-Nupe alliance.

[3] Ajayi, *Christian Missions*, 95–97.

[4] *Ibid.*, XV, 97.

they hoped, would encourage their people to emigrate to their homes in the Niger valley and this in turn would encourage trade and open up new opportunities for their own people similar to the Yoruba mission achievements for the Yoruba people.[1] In their anxiety, the Society had asked the Rev. Edward Jones, a West Indian who was the principal of the Freetown Grammar School, to lead a delegation of three Ibo leaders to the Niger to ascertain how the chiefs would receive them, and to pave the way for a Niger mission.[2] No adequate arrangements were made for their transportation up the Niger and they went by the mail boat to Fernando Po, where they interviewed Consul Beecroft. He dissuaded them from seeking to ascend the Niger by canoes in the absence of a steamer. They found transport to Calabar where, despite some reservations on the part of the Presbyterian missionaries, the Efik rulers assured them of a warm welcome. Then they returned to Freetown without having been able to visit the Niger. The Society therefore grasped the opportunity offered by the *Pleaid* to send Crowther and a few interpreters, including Simon Jonas, the Ibo interpreter of the 1841 Expedition, to explore the feasibility of missionary work on the Niger.

This expedition was to have been led by Beecroft, who had taken so much initiative in the consolidation of the British position along the coast as well as in the exploration of the Niger as the agent of Jamieson and latterly on his own. He died, however, only a few days before the members of the expedition began to assemble at Fernando Po. Crowther paid him some touching compliments in his journal which show the gap between nationalist opinion in his day and ours. Dr. William Balfour Baikie of the Royal Navy, who had been sent as his deputy, medical adviser, and naturalist, stepped in

---

[1] Edward Jones in the *Church Missionary Intelligencer*, IV (1853), 253.

[2] *Ibid.*, 253–259, for the Journal of Jones, April 14 to June 2, 1853, reporting on this expedition.

very ably to fill the gap.[1] He had spent the previous months reading all of the available material on the Niger-Benue region. In place of Beecroft's unrivalled local knowledge, Baikie brought not only the practical abilities of a naval officer, but also unexpected intellectual powers.

Although Crowther remained deferential to Baikie, he was one of the key figures of the Expedition. He was the only clergyman on board. He was regularly consulted on major matters of policy, particularly anything concerned with approaches to the African rulers and peoples. His position became more crucial when Baikie quarrelled with T. C. Taylor, whom Macgregor Laird had put in charge of navigating the *Pleaid*.[2] Baikie found him uncooperative and insufficiently interested in the exploratory work of the Expedition and assumed direct control. He relied rather heavily on Thomas Richards, a Yoruba pilot who had travelled with Beecroft and who knew the river well, and Crowther's support became even more essential thereafter. He was often the spokesman and chief negotiator of the Expedition. Above all, he was the chief communicator between the peoples of the Niger Valley and the officials of the Expedition. With his knowledge of Yoruba, some understanding of Igbo and Hausa, and a keen interest in languages generally, he had an immediate appreciation of whatever he observed or listened to which no other member of the expedition could match. He therefore made it his duty to understand and interpret the local customs, predicaments, and attitudes.

---

[1] William Balfour Baikie, 1825–1864, M.D. Edinburgh, joined the Royal Navy as Surgeon, was appointed to join the *Pleaid* as medical adviser and came to prominence when he had to take over as leader. He later returned to the Niger in 1857–64, when he established himself at Lokoja as unofficial British consul, collecting information about markets, languages, etc. He died on the voyage home. See Christopher C. Ifemesia, "British Enterprise on the Niger," unpub. Ph.D. thesis (London, 1959).

[2] Baikie, *Narrative of an Exploring Voyage*, 91–93, 412–413.

For the scholar, the most valuable part of Crowther's *Journal* relates to the journey on the Benue from the confluence to Garuwa in Muri emirate. Apart from Barth's account of Yola, still unpublished when Crowther wrote, and the word lists in John Clarke's *Specimens of Dialects* and Sigismund Koelle's *Polyglotta*, Crowther's was the first major descriptive account of the Idoma, the Tiv, the Jukun, and the other peoples of the Benue valley.[1] In it are useful recordings of traditional history and other ethnographic data not elsewhere available. Crowther sums up these data in a valuable appendix— "The Countries on the Banks of the Niger and Binue"— written after the Expedition. The greatest merit of the *Journal*, however, is that it gives a day-to-day account of a very fluid historical situation.

Crowther visited the Benue river at a time of rapid political and demographic change, and he gives us a graphic picture of what those changes meant in human terms.[2] The creation of the Sokoto Caliphate has been written about almost exclusively from the Sokoto end. The extent to which the southern frontiers of the Caliphate in Bida, Gombe, Muri, and Adamawa impinged upon the peoples of the middle Niger and Benue regions has never been studied in detail. Whenever this study takes place, Crowther's eye-witness account will be an invaluable supplement and counter-check to oral tradition. Until such a study is undertaken, Crowther's *Journal* remains the most useful account of this crucial

[1] A. H. M. Kirk-Greene (ed.), *Barth's Travels in Nigeria* (Oxford U. P., London, 1962), 172–200; John Clarke, *Specimens of Dialects: Short Vocabularies of Languages and Notes of Countries and Customs in Africa* (Berwick-upon-Tweed, 1848); S. W. Koelle, *Polyglotta Africana* (London, 1854). Koelle's word list came from the Yala dialect at the southern end of Idoma, while Crowther's came from the northern part of Idoma. (Information from R. G. Armstrong.)

[2] Daryll Forde, P. Brown, and R. G. Armstrong, *Peoples of the Niger-Benue Confluence* (London, 1955), p. 57. See also Laura and Paul Bohannan, *The Tiv of Central Nigeria* (London, 1953), and Kirk-Greene, *Adamawa Past and Present*.

aspect of a major revolutionary period of Nigerian
history.

Nevertheless, the predominant significance of
Crowther's *Journal* must be sought in its place in the
history of the expansion of Christianity in Nigeria. With
the basic conclusion that "the time is fully come when
Christianity must be introduced on the banks of the
Niger," Crowther's 1854 *Journal* brought great optimism
to the Society.[1] The welcome that the members of the
expedition—and particularly the Sierra Leoneans—
received, and the avoidance of sickness and death, were
the two principal bases for this optimism. The hostility
of the Delta peoples was played down.[2] For a long time,
too, it was not realised that the emigration of the Ibo and
others to the Niger would never equal that of the Yoruba
in size or significance. No other ethnic group had experienced the mass evacuation that the Yoruba suffered in
the 1820s and 1830s. There was never the same degree of
spontaneous emigration back to their former homes.
Most Ibos in Sierra Leone either did not originally come
from the banks of the Niger or were born in Sierra Leone.
Eventually, when the Society came to rely on Sierra
Leoneans to establish the Niger mission, most of the
missionaries were regarded more as aliens than as exiles
returning home.[3]

Crowther's *Journal* drew attention to the major
centres of future missionary work, not only Aboh, Idah,
and the confluence of the Niger-Benue which had been
earmarked in 1841, but also Asaba and Onitsha, which
Crowther regarded as the most important sites.[4] Crowther
was already sketching out his approach to missionary
work, the lines of which later became very controversial.

[1] See below, xvi.
[2] See below, 10–11.
[3] Ajayi, *Christian Missions*, 41–43.
[4] See below, 180. "Asaba and Onitsha on the opposite shores
present the two most promising localities to be inspected by those
whose lot it may be to commence missionary operations among
the Ibos."

In particular, he argued that one reason why the mission to the Niger must soon be established was the necessity to use the generation of Ibos and others who had lived in the Niger Valley before their enslavement and emancipation. Such people, he wrote, could have an immediate impact on their people and rulers which younger men born and trained abroad could not. The older generation, Crowther insisted, whether or not they were educated in the Western mode, must be in the vanguard of missionary work.[1] The great reliance on such untrained missionaries was to constitute one of the great hazards of the Niger mission, but it is also an important factor in understanding Crowther's missionary techniques.[2]

The greatest importance of Crowther's *Journal* was the further light it threw on Crowther's own abilities and qualities of leadership. Without knowing it, Crowther qualified himself for the leadership of a Niger mission, whenever one was established. It was natural that when Macgregor Laird finally got his contract in 1857 and the first follow up voyage was arranged, Crowther would be asked to accompany it and establish the mission.[3] For the rest of his life, Crowther's centre of activities shifted from Sierra Leone and the Yoruba country to the Niger, particularly to work among the Ijaw, Ibo, Igala, and Nupe peoples.

University of Ibadan   J. F. ADE AJAYI
November 1968

---

[1] See below, xvi–xvii.

[2] Ajayi, *Christian Missions*, 221–223.

[3] S. A. Crowther and J. C. Taylor, *Preaching the Gospel on the Banks of the Niger: Journals of the 1857 Niger Expedition* (London, 1859).

JOURNAL

OF

AN EXPEDITION

UP

THE NIGER AND TSHADDA RIVERS,

UNDERTAKEN

By MACGREGOR LAIRD, Esq.

IN

CONNECTION WITH THE BRITISH GOVERNMENT,

IN 1854.

BY THE

REV. SAMUEL CROWTHER.

WITH MAP AND APPENDIX.

LONDON:

CHURCH MISSIONARY HOUSE, SALISBURY SQUARE;

SEELEY, JACKSON, AND HALLIDAY, FLEET STREET.

MDCCCLV.

CONTENTS.

CHAP. I.

CHAP. II.

CHAP. III.

CHAP. IV.

CHAP. V.

PREFACE.

In the summer of 1853, Macgregor Laird, Esq., a merchant of London, long and extensively engaged in the West African trade, entered into a contract with Her Majesty's Government to fit out and send a small steamer to the river Niger, to ascend the stream to the confluence with the Tshadda, and then to explore that branch of the river. The object of the Expedition was to establish commercial relations with the native tribes: it was also hoped that Dr. Barth, the celebrated African traveller, would be met with in that part of the country.* Her Majesty's Government was to appoint certain officers to accompany the Expedition, and Mr. Laird was to provide for trade and barter with the natives. The risk and main expense of the

---

* About the time when the earlier sheets of *The Journal* were passing through the press, rumours had reached this country that Dr. Barth had lost his life in Africa; and hence the doubt respecting him expressed in a note, which will be found in p. 19. Dr. Barth, happily, has since returned to this country in safety. While the Expedition was up the Tshadda he was at a considerable distance in the interior.

undertaking rested with Mr. Laird, who immediately made to the Committee of the Church
Missionary Society, the generous offer of a free
passage for the Rev. Samuel Crowther, if he
might be allowed to accompany the Expedition.
After communicating with Africa, and ascer-
taining Mr. Crowther's willingness to go, the
Committee thankfully accepted Mr. Laird's offer.
This act of liberality on the part of Mr. Laird,
is only an additional proof of the lively interest
which he has long taken in promoting the best
interests of the natives of Africa.

Mr. Crowther had accompanied the former
Niger Expedition in 1841, under Captain H. D.
Trotter, R.N., of which an account was pub-
lished by the Society, containing the journals
of the Rev. C. F. Schön and Mr. Crowther.
Another member of the present Expedition, Mr.
Simon Jonas, a native Christian, had also ac-
companied the former, as an Interpreter.

The general results of this Expedition, as con-
trasted with all former attempts, are ably stated
in letters written after its return by Mr. Laird
to the Earl of Clarendon, which are with his
Lordship's permission, here inserted.

Mr. Macgregor Laird *to the* Earl of
Clarendon.

3, *Mincing-lane,*
8th Feb., 1855.

My Lord,

I have the honour and pleasure to inform you
that the exploring steam-vessel 'Pleiad,' has safely
returned from the Chadda, after ascending 250
miles beyond the point reached by former Expeditions.

The exploration occupied 118 days, and was un-
accompanied by any loss of life; marking a new era
in African discovery, and showing that by means of
her navigable streams, the interior of that immense
continent, may be safely and economically brought
into relation with the civilized world.

I beg leave to congratulate your Lordship on the
success which has attended an enterprise, promoted
principally by yourself, and trust that that success
will be followed up annually for some years to come,
until the interior of that great continent is fully explored by the countrymen of Park and Clapperton,
under their national flags.

These immense African rivers being now proved
accessible to Europeans under proper management,
and at the proper season with impunity, my object in
offering to contract for the service is attained, and I
must decline proceeding further, as the outlay of

capital necessary is too great a strain upon my private means; and the loss already sustained is quite
as much as I am justified in sacrificing, even for such
an object.

I have the honour to remain,
My Lord,
Your obedient servant,
M. LAIRD.

The Right Hon. Lord Clarendon.

MR. MACGREGOR LAIRD *to the* EARL OF
CLARENDON.

3, *Mincing Lane,*
5th March, 1855.

MY LORD,

THE result of the late ascent of the Chadda
has been so successful in proving the practicability
of exploring Central Africa by her magnificent rivers,
which in all tropical countries, and in Africa especially, are the natural lines of communication, that
I trust Her Majesty's Government will persevere in
following up the geographical discoveries so ably
commenced by Dr. Baikie; and though the expense
and risk has proved too great for me, individually,
to again offer my services on the same terms as
contractor, the interest I take in the subject may
excuse my now addressing your Lordship.

Standing out in broad relief from all former
ascents of the Niger or land expeditions of discovery
into Central Africa, the Chadda exploration is re-

markable for the safe return to this country of all Europeans engaged in it.

In 1805, Mungo Park perished descending the Niger with three companions, the survivors of 38 men who left the Gambia with him.

In 1816 Captain Tuckey's Expedition to the Congo failed, and only one survivor of it reached England.

In 1821 to 1824, Denham and Clapperton's Expedition from the Mediterranean to Soudan, lost its leader, Dr. Oudney, and other Europeans.

In 1825, Clapperton himself, and his companions, Captain Pearce and Dr. Morrison, lost their lives penetrating the Continent from the Bight of Benin, his servant, Richard Lander, being the sole survivor.

In the same year, Major Laing perished after reaching Timbuctoo.

In 1830, Richard and John Lander reached the Niger from Badagry, and floating down the stream, discovered its embouchure on the Bight of Biafra.

In 1832 and 1833, the Liverpool Expedition (the first ascent of the Niger from the sea) took place under my command. We lost 40 out of 49 Europeans.

In 1836, 1840, and 1845, the late Consul Beecroft made the ascents of the Niger with considerable loss of European life on each occasion.

In 1841, the Government Expedition under Captain Trotter, lost, in 62 days, 42 white men out of 150.

The Chadda expedition may be therefore considered to mark a new era in African discovery; the deadly climate having been fairly met and conquered by improved medical treatment and mechanical organization. The plausible objection to exploring Africa—the risk of life—is answered; and the question now is, whether, after the lives of so many gallant men have been sacrificed, during the last half century, in clearing the way, and that way being now proved to be safe and practicable, Her Majesty's Government will, at an expense of a few thousands annually, complete the work of discovery in Central Africa, or allow that honour, which ought to belong to the British race, to be reaped by others.

Whatever ultimately may be the commercial value of the trade of Central Africa, the results of all trading expeditions hitherto have proved its present amount to be not equal to the expense of getting at it. Speaking as a mercantile man, there is no inducement to follow up the trade. For years it must be a losing one; and if after seven or ten years it became profitable, others would reap its benefits equally with the first adventurers.

As to any appreciable effect the continuance of the exploration would have upon the foreign traffic in slaves, *that* depends so much, if not altogether, upon the demand in the Western hemisphere, that annual expeditions for years to come could not possibly affect it.

The reasons I venture to urge upon your Lordship to continue the exploration of Central Africa are, the scientific and geographical results that it is proved may now be realized, at little risk of life, in the unknown countries which extend over 25 degrees of latitude, and 50 degrees of longitude, and which are virgin ground to the traveller. The great importance of keeping up the spirit of enterprize and research in our countrymen, and the advantage we possess in having in the educated African youth in the Colonies of the Gambia, Sierra Leone, and the Gold Coast, most efficient Native agents; by their means new energy and a higher standard of living may be introduced naturally, unobtrusively, and rapidly, into the remotest regions of the interior.

To succeed, this return of the civilized African to his native country, carrying the English habits and language with him, must be spontaneous and self-supporting.

The next point is to make the communication annual and regular, so as to give the people confidence in the periodical visit of a steamer.

I attach great importance to the annual visit of the steamer, as it would prevent the tribes in the Delta stopping the passage of the people above them to the sea—enabling them to open direct communication with the trading vessels at the mouths of the rivers.

From the observations of Dr. Baikie, it would appear the month of June is the best time to enter the Niger. This would require the steamer to leave this country in April, so that if the expedition is to be renewed, an early decision must be come to. I am still of opinion that the best way to carry it on is by contract for a certain number of years. The expense is then fixed, and the contractor has every inducement to encourage the trade, and keep on good terms with the natives. But if the Government wish to carry it on entirely with their own officers, after the experience acquired, and consider the ' Pleiad ' a suitable vessel for the purpose, I will hand her over, at a valuation, on her arrival in the Thames, and give every assistance in my power to forward the enterprize; or if any private individual undertakes it, I will be glad to afford him all the information I possess as to the trade, and if he wishes it, deliver the ' Pleiad ' to him on the same terms.

I take for granted that Her Majesty's Government have no intention of forming any settlement, or interfering with the native powers in Central Africa. I should very much regret if any such attempt was made. The only hope of improving the interior is by African influence, introducing a superior race of negro blood. This can be found to considerable extent in the youth of our own Colonies. They volunteer for the work, and all that is required is to open the way for them. When in the interior they will soon assert their superiority, and may be safely left to take charge of themselves.

I know, my Lord, that it will be said the time is not favourable for a renewal of African expeditions; that other and more vital affairs occupy and engross the attention and mind of the public; but I trust and know that this is not, and never was the true feeling of the great mass of my countrymen. Fifty years back, while engaged in a far severer struggle than the present one, they sent out Mungo Park to explore Central Africa for the pure love of science; and the present generation will as readily support your Lordship in carrying out the work you have commenced.

> I have the honour to remain,
> &c., &c.,
> M. LAIRD.

The Right Hon. Lord Clarendon.

To these letters must be added one from the Rev. S. Crowther, in which he takes a brief review of the Expedition, and makes a forcible appeal on the importance of immediate measures to improve the existing facilities for introducing Civilization and Christianity amongst his countrymen, in the regions of the Niger.

The REV. S. CROWTHER *to the* REV. H. VENN.

> '*Bacchante*,' at Sea,
> Dec. 2, 1854.

REV. AND DEAR SIR,

YOU will, no doubt, be glad to hear that we have returned from the Niger in good health and spirits, — a singular instance, without any death, either among the Europeans, twelve in number, or among the fifty-four Africans, either from sickness or accident. The Expedition was in the river exactly

sixteen weeks, the very day it returned to the mouth
of the Nun. We commenced our ascent of the
Tshadda on the 7th of August, and the last point we
were able to reach was Gurowa, above Bomanda, a
port of Hamaruwa,* about 300 miles from the confluence of the Kowara and Tshadda, on the 22nd
of September, when we were completely short of fuel,
no wood being obtainable within three or four miles
of the banks of the river. This was the only difficulty we met with, and which prevented our reaching the confluence of the Binue and Faro, where it was
crossed by Dr. Barth, and, according to all the accounts we have received, could not have been more
than 100 miles from Hamaruwa. It could be reached
in five days' journey on foot, travelling by the course
of the river, but dangerous on account of unsubdued
natives, and ten days' journey by a circuitous route
around the Fumbina mountains, which was said to
be safer. The reception we met with all along from
the kings and chiefs of the countries on the Binue
was beyond expectation. We made two visits to
Mohamma, the Sultan of Hamaruwa, fourteen miles
from the river, in both which we were most respect-
fully received and entertained by the Sultan.

We returned to Aboh† on the 31st of October,
and met Simon Jonas, whom we had left there, quite
well and much respected by all, both chiefs and
people. He moved about among them with perfect
freedom, and made several visits up the river, to Os-

* Spelt Hamarrua in Mr. Koelle's map.

† Ibo or Aboh, the chief town of the Ibo Tribe, situated on the
upper border of the Delta of the Niger.

e, Onitsha, and Asaba markets, and to an inte-
town called Oko-Ala, on the back of Aboh, of
out a day's journey; the chief of which place asked
Simon Jonas, why we always stopped at Aboh,
and never paid them a visit; to whom Jonas replied,
that there will not be left a place unvisited in due
time. He was about three days absent from Aboh,
when he returned, for fear the steamer might arrive
in his absence.

Simon Jonas spoke to them of the folly of their
superstitious customs, and he said, the one of chewing stick to clean their teeth early in the morning,
and spouting the spittle before their country fashion,
invoking his blessing upon those who wish them good,
and imprecating his anger upon those who desire
their hurt, was given up by some of them at his
speaking to them of the folly of so doing. He was
the companion of Tshukuma and Aje, although he
paid them due respect.

Having found this favourable state of things in
Aboh, I took the step to secure a parcel of ground for
a contemplated Mission station, to prevent the spot
being spoiled by the people, and gave Aje strict
charge to keep the people away from it. My further
proceedings in Aboh will be seen more fully in my
journal to that place. I have furnished the Bishop
of Sierra Leone with a copy of my journals to Aboh
for his fuller information; and I have suggested to
Dr. Baikie the advantage of taking Simon Jonas to
Sierra Leone, to give his Lordship verbal information
of Aboh country from actual knowledge of three
months stay among them. I have taken these steps

from the instruction I had received from the B...
to ascertain what reception Native Teachers w...
meet with in Aboh should any be sent there.

I regret much that none of those who accompanied Mr. Jones* to the same place for the same
object had been sent with the Expedition.

I believe the time is fully come when Christianity
must be introduced on the banks of the Niger : the
people are willing to receive any who may be sent
among them. The English are still looked upon as
their friends, with whom they themselves desire to
have connexion as with the first nation in the world.
Could the work have been begun since 1841, how
imperfect soever it might have been, yet it would
have kept up the thread of connexion with England
and the countries on the banks of the Niger. God
has provided instruments to begin the work, in the
liberated Africans in the Colony of Sierra Leone,
who are the natives of the banks of this river.

If this time is allowed to pass away, the generation of the liberated teachers who are immediately
connected with the present generation of the natives
of the interior will pass away with it also; many
intelligent men who took deep interest in the introduction of trade and Christianity by the Niger,
who had been known to the people, have died since ;
so have many of the chiefs and people in the country,
who were no less interested to be brought in connexion with England by seeing their liberated coun-

* The Rev. E. Jones, with three natives of the Ibo Tribe in
Sierra Leone, attempted to reach the Ibo country in April, 1853,
but found it unsafe to ascend the Niger without a steamer. *Vide*
" Church Missionary Intelligencer," November 1853.

ymen return. Had not Simon Jonas been with us,
who was well known to Obi and his sons, we should
have had some difficulty in gaining the confidence of
the people at Aboh at our ascent.

It would be of very great advantage if the colony-
born young men were introduced by their parents or
countrymen to their fatherland; it has many advantages which have not been sufficiently noticed. It
cannot be expected that children born in the Colony
should become acquainted with the countries and
characters of the people so soon as their parents and
countrymen. Though the parents are illiterate, yet
if they are sincere followers of the Lord Jesus Christ,
their service will be of much worth in introducing
Christianity to their own people. They are brought
back to their country as a renewed people, looked
upon by their countrymen as superior to themselves,
as long as they continue consistent in their Christian
walk and conversation, and do not disgrace themselves by following heathenish practices. The language of the people of Abbeokuta will be that of the
natives on the banks of the Niger : "Let those who
come from the white man's country teach us and
condemn our heathenish practices, we shall listen to
them." It takes great effect when returning liberated
Christians sit down with their heathen countrymen,
and speak with contempt of their own former superstitious practices, of whom, perhaps, many now alive
would bear testimony as to their former devotedness
in their superstitious worship ; all which he now can
tell them he has found to be foolishness, and the
result of ignorance; when he with all earnestness,

invites them, as Moses did Hobab, Come with us, for the Lord has promised good to Israel : and all this in his own language, with refined Christian feelings and sympathy, not to be expressed in words, but evidenced by an exemplary Christian life. The services of such persons will prove most useful in the introduction of the Gospel of Jesus Christ among the heathens. Let such persons be employed as readers or Christian visitors, and thus they will gradually introduce their children into the country, who in course of time will be able to carry on the work more effectually ; as pioneers, we must not look for instruments of the keenest edge, anything that will open the path for future improvement will answer as well at the onset.

*   *   *

I shall entrust my journals to the care of Dr. Baikie, made up into a parcel with some specimens of translation of Doma or Arago language, and that of the Mitshis, not found among Koelle's collection. I have also sent under his care a long red box, containing curiosities from the river, which I hope will safely reach you.

I remain,

Rev. and dear Sir, &c.

SAMUEL CROWTHER.

DR. BAIKIE *to the* REV. S. CROWTHER.

Clarence, Fernando Po,
November 28, 1854.

MY DEAR MR. CROWTHER,

After having been together for upwards of four months, closely engaged in exploring Central Africa, I cannot allow you to depart without expressing to you, in the warmest manner, the pleasure I derived from your company, and acknowledging the information I have reaped from you.

Your long and intimate acquaintance with native tribes, with your general knowledge of their customs, peculiarly fit you for a journey such as we have now returned from, and I cannot but feel that your advice was always readily granted to me, nor had I ever the smallest reason to repent having followed it. It is nothing more than a simple fact, that no slight portion of the success we met with in our intercourse with the tribes is due to you.

*　　　　*　　　　*

Our voyage has providentially terminated so far favourably, and without loss of life.

You are now about to return to the scene of your past labours, and to resume your share of the work for civilizing and regenerating a vast territory. That your labours may continue to meet with success, and that you may be spared to see your exertions bearing good fruit, is the earnest and sincere wish of

Yours very faithfully,

W. B. BAIKIE.

The prospects opened by this Expedition acquire an additional interest when viewed in connexion with the extension of the Yoruba Mission, which has already reached several large towns, connected by intercourse with the tribes on the banks of the Niger, at various points, extending many hundred miles from its Delta. In a journal, just received from Mr. Crowther, after his return to this Mission, he thus notices his visit to Ibadan, which is the most Easterly of the towns at present occupied by the Missionaries of this Society.

EXTRACT FROM THE JOURNAL OF THE REV. SAMUEL CROWTHER.

Jan. 1855.

" I told Bôlle, the chief of Ibadan, that I had lately returned from the Niger, and that I had heard of his soldiers being with Dasaba, in that neighbourhood. He replied—Yes, that there were about 1,000 Ibadan soldiers with him. I said, had we made arrangements to that effect previous to our ascent up the Tshadda, I would have returned by way of Rabba or Lade, with his warriors, through Yoruba to Ibadan. He said, certainly, that I could have done so, and that it might be done now from here to Rabba and Lade, on the banks of the Niger. With prudent management and means to effect it, how easily the road could be opened across the Yoruba country to the Niger! The opportunity should be

embraced when we can get the aid of the chiefs in
accomplishing such an object : it is much better to
act in co-operation with them, than without them—
they know their own interest in having Europeans
for their friends, and with a little encouragement
they can be made use of in effecting much in this
country.

The disposition of the people at Ibadan though
warlike, yet is not unfavourable to peace and trade ;
they are not worse than the Egbas of Abbeokuta,
and I have seen even at Ibadan the effect of the
establishment of lawful trade at Lagos. Palm oil,
with which Ibadan abounds, is a chief article of
trade at this time, large calabashes full are conveyed
through the Ijebu country to the coast, and others
find their way to Abbeokuta, where it is sold to the
Egbas, who convey it to Lagos, in their numerous
canoes, by the Ogun river.

Cotton is another staple article of trade, which will
largely occupy the attention of the people in general
in this country : the extent of farms now under cultivation in cotton and other produce, though merely
for home consumption, was not known in Ibadan
for many years back. How much will it be extended
if they are a little encouraged, and a market is
opened for their cotton.

In order to take full advantage of the present
opportunity, it is evident, as Mr. Laird has pointed out, that Her Majesty's Government should
assist in keeping open this great river-road into
the interior of Africa, at least for a few years :

until the natives themselves shall become sufficiently sensible of the advantages of lawful commerce and the benefits of Christian Teachers, so
as to co-operate, as among the Yoruba tribes, in
maintaining a friendly intercourse with their European benefactors.   A meeting of a few of the
influential friends of Africa has been already held
in London, in July last, to confer with Dr.
Baikie upon this subject—Sir T. D. Ackland,
Bart., M.P., in the chair, at which the following
Resolutions were adopted :—

That it appears to this Meeting that the opportunities of introducing civilization and Christianity into
Africa, by the navigation of the rivers Niger and
Tshadda, contemplated in the Expedition of 1841,
are shown to be still most promising by the late Expedition of 1854, and that they should be promptly
improved by this country before they are closed by
any change of circumstances, or taken out of our
hands by other nations.

That it is essential to the success of any plans for
the attainment of this object by means of Native
agency, that Her Majesty's Government should establish or promote the establishment of a regular steam
communication between Fernando Po and the confluence of the Niger and Tshadda rivers, in order that
Native Traders may be assured that the way will be
kept open; and also that Her Majesty's Government
should, at periodical intervals, extend such communication further up the two rivers, with a view to the

extension of geographical discovery, of commercial enterprize, and of religious civilization in the interior of Africa.

That should Her Majesty's Government accede to this proposal, there is every prospect of the completion of the great and benevolent object in view, by the spontaneous commercial enterprise of liberated and other Africans in the various settlements upon the West Coast, and by the zeal of Missionary Societies.

The Board of Admiralty have kindly sanctioned the insertion of a Map of the course of the rivers, reduced by Mr. Arrowsmith from a larger Admiralty Chart, furnished by the Naval Officers attached to the Expedition.

May the good hand of the Lord, which is evidently beckoning us forward in our efforts to reach these long isolated members of the human family, and to bring them within the circle of Christian civilization, direct and prosper all the measures which may be adopted for this end, and may He shortly establish His kingdom in this long-benighted region.

Church Missionary House,
October, 1855.

JOURNAL,

&c. &c.

CHAP. I.

June 13, 1854. To-day, being the day I had
fixed upon to start for Lagos, preparatory to my
joining the Expedition to explore the Tshadda,
Messrs. Townsend, Maser, and King, and Dr. Irving,
kindly came over to bid me farewell. After Mr.
Townsend had offered up a prayer for God's protection and guidance, about eight A.M. I left Abbeokuta with Mr. Phillip and my son Samuel, who were
also going down to Lagos; many of my church
members followed me to Agbamaya. I took about
seven hundred-weight of clean cotton down with
me, to be shipped for Manchester.

June 15: Started early this morning from
Agboyi, where we stopped last night, and arrived
at Lagos about half-past eight A.M. Here I was
sorry to hear of the unexpected illness of Mr. Beecroft, and that he was about to leave for Teneriffe
by the next mail from Fernando Po.

June 17 : The 'Bacchante' arrived this morning from Fernando Po, and brought the painful intelligence of Mr. Beecroft's death, which took place the night before she sailed. I felt this very much as the Expedition was just expected, and I knew no other person connected with it besides him ; this caused a little anxiety, but I resigned everything to God's good and unerring providence.

June 18 : *Sunday.* Attended morning service in Mr. Gollmer's church, and in the afternoon at Mr. White's house, where I heard Mr. Phillip address the congregation.

June 19 : To-day was spent in making necessary preparations, and writing letters for England, against the arrival of the mail.

June 20 : The 'Forerunner' arrived about one o'clock P.M., by which I learnt that some of the gentlemen of the Expedition were on board of her, and that the 'Pleiad' would not touch at Lagos, but proceed. direct to Fernando Po, so I prepared myself for embarking to-morrow morning.

June 21 : About nine A.M., I embarked, and was very glad to meet Dr. Baikie, Dr. Bleek, and Mr. Dalton, a young zoological assistant, on board ; they kindly brought me letters from England and Sierra Leone, and parcels of books and many useful articles from Lady Buxton and Captain Trotter, for which I was very thankful. I was sorry to find Dr. Bleek rather out of health, but it was thought he might be better by the time we arrived at Fernando Po. There was also on board, the Rev. J. Diboll, with Mrs. Diboll and daughter, Baptist

missionary to Fernando Po: they were all very glad
to see me. About half-past eleven A.M. the 'Forerunner' weighed anchor, and in a short time we
lost sight of Lagos.

June 22; Arrived off the Bonny river, where
a ship was lying at anchor; the mail was left in
charge of one of the passengers, who left the 'Forerunner', and went on board of her: she was waiting
for the pilot to take her across the bar next morning;
we made for Old Calabar. After crossing the bar
we anchored for the night.

June 23: Arrived at Old Calabar about eleven
A.M; as the mail was only to stop here a few hours
I could not go on shore to advantage. Mr. W. C.
Thompson, son of the late Mr. W. C. Thompson,
linguist, in connection with the Church Missionary
Society at Sierra Leone, took his passage in her
for England, and the missionaries accompanied him
on board ; about four o'clock P.M. we started, and
anchored outside the bar.

June 24 : Arrived at Cameroon river about
seven P.M. The mails were delivered, and received
that night.

June 25: *Sunday.* Started as soon as it was
light, and made for Fernando Po. It rained heavily;
in consequence of which no service could be held.
About four P.M. we anchored off Clarence, and found
to our great disappointment that the 'Pleiad' had not
yet arrived : various thoughts were expressed and
conjectures made, as may be expected, as to the cause
of her non-arrival. I landed, and took my lodging
at Mr. J. Wilson's, the same house I occupied in

1841 with Mr. Schön, in which we held divine service during our stay in the island. The people were very glad to see me, and expressed their regret for the loss of Mr. Beecroft; for he had made full preparation for the Expedition; and had engaged many intelligent natives who had been used to go up the Niger with him, and who were ready to go anywhere with him, they being mutually attached to each other, for he treated them as a father. It will be a long time before his place can be supplied by another, who will take the same interest in the country and her people as he did.

June 26: Took my boxes on shore to my lodging; every one was on the look out for the 'Pleiad'. After breakfast, visited Mr. Beecroft's grave, which is on the point of the cliff of Clarence, under a large cotton-tree, where he himself had directed that he should be buried. Thus ended the life of this useful person, after twenty-five years stay in Africa, during which period he had won the affection of many who knew his worth in the countries he had visited; and could not but greatly regret to hear of his removal by death. The chiefs of Abbeokuta had sent salutations and messages to him by me, which he did not live to receive. As long as this generation lasts, the name of Mr. Beecroft will not be forgotten in this part of West Africa.

June 27: The 'Pleiad' had not arrived, and the 'Forerunner' would not have waited any longer, had not Captain Miller, senior officer of Her Majesty's squadron in the Bights, ordered her to stay till Thursday.

June 28 : The 'Pleiad' arrived this evening, to the great joy of all parties.

June 29 : The 'Forerunner' had been detained two days beyond her time, or she would have towed the 'Pleiad' off the Nun, in order to save fuel; she sailed away this evening with our letters for England. Dr. Bleek's state of health being considered by the medical gentlemen to be very precarious, he was pronounced unfit to accompany the Expedition, and was consequently sent back to England by the 'Forerunner.'

July 2: *Sunday.* Held the morning service in Mr. Beecroft's new house, which Mr. Lynslager had kindly ordered to be cleared out yesterday for the purpose : the service was well attended, both by resident Europeans and many from the ships in the cove, besides many of the Native settlers in connection with the Baptist Church; Captain Miller, of the 'Crane' was also present. I preached from 2 Cor. v. 1.

July 3—7 : Captain Miller rendered every possible assistance to hasten the departure of the 'Pleiad', and as his help was no more needed, he sailed away to-day.

July 8 : This afternoon, I embarked on board the 'Pleiad', as she was to sail this evening. About nine P.M. we weighed for the Nun, with two large iron canoes laden with coals in tow; the friends who accompanied us a short distance from the harbour left us with hearty cheers. As the wind rose, and the swell became heavy, the canoes did not tow well, and there was some fear of their being upset: the night was, therefore, past with some anxiety.

July 9: *Sunday.* Heavy rains: we were not much more than twenty miles from Fernando Po. The canoes continued to labour from the heavy swell and a strong current; the steamer could not go more than half her speed for fear of swamping the canoes. About noon, the spindle of the safety-valve gave way, and steam could not be kept up, so we could not proceed until it was repaired, which took three hours, and we were drifted eastward by the westerly current, with heavy swell and rains. Nearly all hands were sea-sick, no service could be held.

July 10: Off the mouth of the Bonny river; our progress very slow; the safety-valve out of order, in consequence of which we were many times short of steam.

July 11: Off the mouth of the St. John or Brass river; anchored for the night between it and the mouth of the Nun.

July 12: About two P.M. with the flood tide we crossed the bar;* the 'Pleiad' was piloted by Mr. Thomas Richards, a Yoruba man, who had made many voyages up the Niger with the late Mr. Beecroft, and has a good knowledge of the localities about the coast and the Niger. When we were in the midst of the bar, the hawser of one of the canoes, in which there were seven Krumen, broke, and as

---

* In the former Expedition this same bar was crossed one month later in the year, viz. August 13th: and a week was spent before the vessels began to ascend the river. ED.

we could not stop to render her any assistance, she was left to make the best of her way through the surf, though not without great anxiety for the men; for the surf was tremendous, so much so that it broke once over our poop, though the tide was in our favour: every eye was fixed upon the drifted canoe, and it was no small joy to see her now and then buoyed up from the deep furrow upon the top of the surf, following our track, till she got across in safety:—the iron canoes seem to ride very lightly upon the surf. About three o'clock we anchored inside the bar very near to Alburka Island: when the engineer came to examine the engine, he found that the safety-valve was just gone, and it was providential that we had got across the bar before this happened.

July 13, 14: These days were spent in repairing the engine; and on the 15th, about six A.M., we got under weigh for the Niger. Louis' Creek was found blocked up, so Mr. Richards took a boat to sound the next creek, the 'Pleiad' waiting at the entrance. He returned about half-past nine A.M., and reported that he had found the channel. We started, with the tide still in our favour; but about twelve o'clock we missed the right channel, and ran aground on the point of Sunday Island, the left passage having been taken instead of the right, which was the proper channel; we could not get the vessel off this evening.

July 16: *Sunday.* With the flood tide exertions were made, and the vessel was hove off about half-past eleven A.M.; but before the ship could be put to rights, it was too late to make any progress. I had service in the afternoon about two o'clock, and preached from St. John i. 22, 23. All hands well and cheerful. When we were lying aground this morning, a canoe was seen paddled down the river with produce; another came alongside with four men in, unarmed, to see the ship, they asked whether she was a slave or oil ship:—they were answered 'palm-oil ship.'

July 17 : We got under weigh about seven A.M. and made good progress in three to seven fathoms water. Soon after we had cleared Sunday Island, traces of cultivation began to appear, together with land about three feet above the water's edge. As the water has not yet risen to its full height, it gave an entirely new appearance to the river, from that it bore in August 1841. At that time, only a few spots near the water's edge were under cultivation, and the whole was covered with water, as the river overflowed its banks. Not only old plantations showed a continued industry of the people of the Delta, but many newly-cleared spots, in the midst of which numerous lofty palm trees stood, which were carefully preserved for their rich and valuable produce, showed further, the improved state of the banks. About three hours from Sunday Island, we came to inhabited villages; we induced two canoes to come off, from whom we learnt that the people between Brass and Aboh are called Oru. One of the people who came off, and who spoke the Ibo language, was so confident, that he offered to go with us to Aboh; and the people on shore, never showed the least sign of opposition, but folded their arms and gazed at the steamer as she glided on. Fewer traces of cultivation were observed during the day till we came to the village of Angiama. Brass people come up· here to buy palm-oil with large casks in their canoes, some of which they land as they proceed upwards. There is another striking change in the habits of the people themselves; in 1841, very few of them were to be found with any decent articles of clothing; I spied to-day, among a group of about forty people on shore, fifteen who I could distinctly see had English shirts on. This is an evident mark of the advantage of legal trade over that in men. The chief of Angiama, or Anya, came off, and expressed his regret, that we did not wait at his village, as Captain Trotter had done; and it was with some difficulty that we could satisfy him by our excuses; but we hoped to be able to stay on our return. Dr. Baikie gave him a red cap and a looking-glass; but I could read in his coun-tenance, as well as by the temper one of his men manifested, that, if they had had it in their power, they would have detained us in Oru, to reap all the benefits of the trade to themselves, instead of allowing it to pass through their waters to the people of the interior beyond them. To-day's voyage occu-pied eleven and a half hours.

Since we entered the Nun, I have been thinking what could have made this river more unhealthy than any other, independent of the general un-healthiness of the climate. It occurred to me, that the evil might have partly originated in the Expedition itself, as nothing had been left undone, especially in 1841, to ensure good health : that, probably, miasma may have been created by the raw and green wood for fuel kept in the bunkers for days together, and by the noxious exudation and vapour issuing therefrom, and by the mixture of chips and bark with the bilge water. I hinted this idea to Captain Taylor, Dr. Baikie, and Dr. Hutchinson, that a trial might be made of keeping the wood in the canoes, and only calling for it as occasion required : they all at once agreed to take every precaution which might be likely to conduce to health.

July 18 : Got under weigh at seven A.M., and steamed past many villages on both banks; several canoes came off. The banks were about six feet above the water's edge, at intervals, on both sides ; one is not impressed with the idea of a swamp by the sight of these high banks. The wind was fresh and pleasant. About noon, we were opposite a group of villages on the left bank, where a creek with plenty of water entered the main river ; we followed it up about half-an-hour, but as it grew narrow and covered with green stuff and weeds, we returned; the natives also told us that it was not the way to king Obi. As we were returning, we met two canoes which were following us, waving a white piece of cloth as a sign of peace. It appears this signal is well known all along the river, and a great way into the interior. They told us that the creek led into the bush, and into a very narrow passage, which they called a hole. They received some trifling presents. About three o'clock we were opposite the villages of Kalabal and Okoloba, where in 1841 the 'Wilberforce' re-entered the main river, and a note was left for the 'Albert's' information. * Here we met a number of Brass people, traders in palm-oil; they came alongside to sell live stock and provisions.

July 19 : Got under weigh about six A.M. Our progress was rather slow, owing to a strong current. About noon we touched the ground on a point below Truro Island, and were about an hour in getting the vessel off; at a short distance, the channel being missed above Truro Island, we ran aground again in the afternoon, where we stayed for the night. Several canoes came off: we asked them respecting Obi, whose death was confirmed, and it was stated that Aje, one of his sons, was now in his father's room, but not recognised as his successor, until white men should come up and decide who should be king. This unexpected intelligence appears favourable as regards the confidence they have in white men. It gave us time to think what it would be best to do, should the matter be brought before the commissioned officer for advice.

July 20 : We remained aground until five P.M., and thus lost a day's voyage. Some of the neighbouring chiefs of Oru came off, with whom we had conversation about legal trade, and in order to get it well established, we pointed out to them the necessity of agreeing among themselves, never to molest English boats or canoes passing up and down the river, as that would prove detrimental to

---

* See Schön and Crowther's Journal, p. 279.

trade, and turn to their own disadvantage. Mr.
Richards, who went to take the soundings this
morning, returned in the afternoon, and confirmed
the statement of the people; he had been told higher
up, that they were waiting the arrival of the white
men who should decide who was to succeed king
Obi.

July 21 : We left at six A.M., and anchored off
Aboh* at five P.M.   The river has fallen considerably
since June, as there has been no rain ; we had some
showers and a few wet days, but not sufficient to
effect a change in the rise of the river; but, however, there was always sufficient water if the channel
were carefully traced out. The 'Pleiad' drew more
than seven feet water.   A great number stood at
each village as we steamed past them, to gaze at
the motion of the ship; they missed the paddles, the
'Pleiad' being a screw ship, (which seemed to answer
remarkably well,) so that the astonished villagers
could not account for the power which propelled
her onward against the strong current.

The people of Aboh showed still some timidity, on
account of the affair of the late Mr. Carr, concerning
whom the 'Wilberforce' came to make some enquiries.†   When Mr. Beecroft last visited this place,

---

* In the journals of the former expedition, this name is written
"Ibo." Ibo, or Igbo, is the name of a large country; Aboh is
a district and town situated in Ibo.

† Mr. Carr accompanied the expedition in 1841, to super-
intend the model farm at the Confluence, and was zealously
labouring there for a short time, when he was taken ill with fever.
The medical men deemed it necessary to take him on board the

I believe in 1845, he went on shore to invite people
on board before any would come off; and as they
had been informed by mistake that he died three
years ago, they did not know who the captain was,
hence their shyness to come to the ship. After
some hesitation, a canoe with five men came off to
us with two yams, which were bought for one empty
bottle : other canoes kept close to the beach at a
great distance. The men who sold the two yams
appeared to be strangers from Oru, and could not
speak Ibo well. On their return, they brought an

" Albert," on her return to Fernando Po. There he was soon
restored to health, and being anxious to return to his post, he
proposed to leave Fernando Po for the river Bonny, and proceed
to the Confluence, by hiring a native canoe and crew. And
when her Majesty's ship " Pluto " left for that river, he availed
himself of the opportunity, and took a passage in her, together
with his native servant. At Bonny he succeeded in obtaining a
boat manned by some men who were strangers at the place, and
who promised to take him as far as Aboh. They left, but from
that time nothing more was heard of Mr. Carr, nor of his servant,
and there can be no doubt, but they were murdered·for the
sake of plunder. Some articles of clothing, seen either at Aboh
or near it, supposed to have belonged to Mr. Carr, gave rise to
the suspicion, that Obi had been implicated in the matter. The
good feeling previously existing between him and the British
officers was interrupted, and some acts of hostility committed on
both sides. From Mr. Crowther's remarks we may gather, that
those unpleasant feelings had not quite subsided, and that but
for the good services and explanations of Simon Jonas, the
expedition might have met with some obstacles at Aboh. The
officers of the present expedition are convinced that Obi had
no concern in Mr. Carr's death. I have always believed, that
if Mr. Carr had reached Aboh, he would have been safe in
Obi's hands ; and that, if he met with a violent death, it took
place, in all probability, soon after his departure from Bonny.
The late Mr. Beecroft entertained the same opinion.—*J. F. Schön.*

Aboh man alongside, who was evidently sent to see who we were. He would not come on board. Simon Jonas was therefore sent in their canoe to inform the chief that we were come. Before he reached the creek, a Haussa man, who was an old servant of Mr. Lander, named after himself (Aliheli Lander), was sent to inquire who we were, and to say that the chief was disappointed that the captain did not *fire* to announce his arrival. Aliheli accompanied Mr. Lander to Fernando Po and back, speaks English, and was subsequently employed by Mr. Beecroft in his voyages up the river, and is well known to many people where the vessels touched. He was slave to king Obi, but got his liberty at his master's death, as it appears, for his good services to him.

From Aliheli, we learnt correctly that since Obi's death there has been some dispute as to his successor. There is another party besides the line of Obi, Osai's family, which lays claim to the throne ; that is the line of Oshiodapara. Obi's eldest son, who has a right to the throne, is Tshukŭma, otherwise called Okorobi, but he appears to lack energy, so that Aje his younger brother, an active man, took the lead, as it appears, with the approbation of Tshukŭma : but the line of Oshiodapara contended for the throne in favour of one Orisè,* and demanded that if Obi's family would not give place to that of Oshiodapara, whatever they had paid to Obi as their king should be returned : so it appears the matter rests at present. Aje heads one party of the town, called

* The final *e* pronounced as a broad open vowel.

the king's party, and Orisè the other party, called Oshiodapara's party. It appears both parties are at peace. Unfortunately Aje and Orisè were not at home on our arrival, but absent at Igara, to which place they had gone some ten days before, to settle some dispute which had taken place between the Atta's subjects, on which occasion, a woman of Oshiodapara's family was accidently killed. We sent Simon Jonas* to tell Tshukŭma that we intended to pay him a visit the next morning.

July 22: Took an early breakfast, and about eight A.M. we started for the town of Aboh, which lies about one mile in length along the western bank of the creek, very thickly populated. We landed close to Tshukŭma's house, which was very small and confined; his old house having been lately burnt. He had been worshipping his god that morning, which we saw in his piazza, in a calabash placed in the front of a wall, covered with a white sheet. We waited about ten minutes before Tshukŭma made his appearance, dressed in a pair of thin Turkish trousers, a white shirt, a white waistcoat, and a string of coral beads about his neck: he is smaller in size and stature than Obi, his father, is very soft in his manners, and seems not possessed of much energy. He shook us all heartily by the hand, and in a short time the little square was crowded to excess, so that there was no room to move; and the place became so thronged, that it was difficult to keep one's seat on the mat spread for our accommodation. Tshukŭma

---

* Simon Jonas is a native of the country, and was employed in the Expedition of 1841.

used all his efforts to command silence, but to no
purpose. Obi's daughter and the chiefs' wives took
their turn to command silence, but it only increased
the noise. At last, Tshukŭma requested us to frighten
the people away, which of course we did not do.
As it was impossible to obtain perfect silence,
I suggested to Dr. Baikie to begin business, as we
could manage to keep close enough to hear each
other.

The substance of Dr. Baikie's interview with
the chief was, that the Queen had desired him to
visit them, and see how they did; that we were
sorry to hear of Obi's death; we hoped his successor would be of the same mind as the late king,
and that they still adhered to the treaty he had
signed with Captain Trotter, who acted in the name
of the Queen; and that trade was now come to the
Aboh country, about which Dr. Hutchinson would
speak fully with him. Tshukŭma replied, that he
was very glad to see a large ship come to Aboh
again, and that he and the other headmen were particularly charged by Obi, before his death, not to
deviate from the path he had trod, respecting his
friendship with the white men, and that they would
act accordingly; but as Aje was absent from home,
in Igara, with a great number of the headmen, to
settle some matter in that place, he expressed a wish
that we would wait till they returned, as he expected
them in three or four days' time, and he would send
a canoe to hasten their return. To this we objected,
because we were in a hurry to go up to fetch down
some white men, who were waiting for us in the

interior.* Tshukŭma said, the fault was not with
them, but with the white men themselves; that many
times promises of trade had been made to them, but
never fulfilled. I told him that the English had it
much in their mind to fulfil their word, but could
not do so till now on account of sickness. Tshukŭma
replied, Had they not gone further than Aboh, they
would not have been taken ill, and been obliged to
return to the sea so soon as they were.

I now thought it time to introduce the subject
of a Missionary establishment among them. I told
him that we had come to see what we could do to
make a Missionary station at Aboh, as we had done in
my country at Badagry, Lagos, and Abbeokuta, and
has been done also at Calabar and the Camaroons.
One of Obi's daughters replied, that they could not
conceive why white men should build houses in
Bonny and Calabar, and not in Aboh? I told them
that our superiors have been thinking of it a long
time, but now they are in earnest, and are very
desirous of sending some Ibo teachers to Aboh, to
reside there, and teach them many things, if they
are willing to learn. Tshukŭma said, my words were
too good for them to hope that they will be realised,
and that he would not believe any thing until he
had seen us do what we proposed; that there was
no difficulty on their part, nor need we fear any

---

* When the Expedition left England, it was hoped that Dr.
Barth and Dr. Vogel, who have penetrated Africa from the
north, might have been able to meet the 'Pleiad.' But subsequent accounts have shown that neither of them could have
been in that neighbourhood at the time, even if Dr. Barth still
survives.

unwillingness to receive those who may be sent to
them or learn what they may be taught; but that
the fault rests with us in not fulfilling what we
promised to do.

To show that I was in earnest in what I had
said, I told him that I would leave Simon Jonas with
him till our return, and that when Aje and the other
chiefs came back, we would talk the matter over
more fully. He was very glad to hear of my intention to leave Simon Jonas with them. After this, we
asked his permission to walk about the town. He
himself accompanied us to Aje's house, which was more
capacious, drier, and better built than his own, in
squares. We sat down there a while, on mats spread
on the floor for us, and soon after left for the town.
The river was greatly fallen, in consequence of which,
the only street which runs parallel with the creek was
free from water, but moist, and it gave us the advantage of walking to a considerable distance, crossing
many gutters formed by the washing of the earth of
the cross streets into the creek. In this long street,
canoes are paddled to the very doors of the houses
at high water. It is very much to be regretted that
such a thickly-populated place as this is not better
situated; however, this should not be an objection to
answer the call, "Come over and help us;" their
willingness to receive teachers, and to be instructed,
amounts to such a call. The chief said, I should
see at my return the driest spot which would answer
our purpose. Tshukŭma being invited on board, he
returned home to make ready, and we returned to
the ship about half-past ten A.M. A short time after,

the chief came on board, accompanied by his head
.wife, Aje's head wife, and three of Obi's daughters.
Captain Taylor had some talk with him about trade,
and took him, and his male and female followers to the
saloon, where they were invited to lunch, which they
seemed to enjoy very much; after this, Dr. Baikie
gave presents to himself and to his female attendants.
He engaged to cut wood for us, which he promised
we should receive in the afternoon, but he was unable
to fulfil his promise, on account of the short notice,
and his people not being near at hand. Tshukŭma
never mentioned that there was any dispute among
them relative to their politics; so we, of course,
appeared ignorant of the matter, but the frequent
mention of the king's party confirmed the report of
the existence of differences among them.

July 23: *Sunday.* Had service on board at half-
past ten, and preached from St. John i. 29. The
boat was just ready for me after service, to go on
shore to see and speak a few words with the chief
on religious subjects, and also to ask his permission
to address the people in the town, when his canoe
appeared from the creek, with numerous attendants,
so I postponed my going till his return; but he remained so long on board, that there was no prospect
of his soon going away. When Captain Taylor had
done with him, I took the opportunity to speak with
him at length on the subject of the Christian religion,
Simon Jonas interpreting for me. The quickness
with which he caught my explanation of the all-
sufficient sacrifice of Jesus Christ, the Son of God,
for the sin of the world, was gratifying. I en-

deavoured to illustrate it to him in this simple way. "What would you think of any persons, who, in broad daylight like this, should light their lamps to assist the brilliant rays of the sun to enable them to see better?" He said, "It would be useless; they would be fools to do so." I replied, "Just so;" that the sacrifice of Jesus Christ, the Son of God, was sufficient to take away our sins, just as one sun is sufficient to give light to the whole world: that the worship of country fashions, and numerous sacrifices, which shone like lamps, only on account of the darkness of their ignorance and superstition, though repeated again and again, yet cannot take away our sins: but that the sacrifice of Jesus Christ, once offered, alone can take away the sin of the world. He frequently repeated the names, "Oparra Tshuku! Oparra Tshuku!" Son of God! Son of God! As I did not wish to tire him out, I left my discourse fresh in his mind. The attention of his attendants, with the exception of a few, was too much engaged in begging and receiving presents, to listen to all I was talking about. I gave Tshukŭma a Yoruba primer, in which I wrote his name; and left some with Simon Jonas, to teach the children, or any who should feel disposed to learn, the Alphabet and words of two letters. Tshukŭma and his attendants were perfectly at home in the steamer, and it was not till a gentle hint was given them, that the gentlemen wanted to take their dinner, that he ordered his people to make ready for their departure, at half-past four o'clock. He desired Simon Jonas to accompany him in his canoe, but I told him that I would send him afterwards. He gave Captain Taylor one bullock, seventy yams, and two hundred pieces of fire-wood. Simon Jonas was sent on shore in the evening with a supply of four thousand cowries and seven fathoms of cloth, for his subsistence till our return.

July 24: Could not start this morning till nine o'clock, in consequence of having lost a kedge with a hawser, the latter rather an indispensable article; after nearly three hours' fruitless search, we moved onward on our voyage. Our progress was very slow to-day. In consequence of the strong current, we missed the channel and got into shoal water, touched twice, and were obliged to drop back, and anchored below Bullock Island. Mr. Richards went to find the channel. We passed a few villages on the right side of the river, and some large canoes from the market passed alongside of us. The country was open here, and the wind was fresh and pleasant.

July 25: Got under weigh at about six A.M., and came opposite the group of villages of Ossamare or Awsimini, on the left bank. This place is said to be the resort of traders between Aboh and the Elugu and Isoama tribes of the Ibo country. If this be correct, taking also the open state of the country from this locality and upwards into consideration, it presents one of the best situations for a Missionary establishment among the Iboes. I shall make it a point to land and learn more of this place on our return. The great number of people along the bank to look at the steamer, tells the thickly populated state of this part of the country; and a great

number of well-looking bullocks which were seen on
the sand-beach, a little distance from those groups of
spectators, speaks in favour of the industry of the
people.   I believe that from this the Bullock Island
took its name.   Steaming was slow and tedious,
owing to a strong current and zigzag passage from
point to point to avoid shallow water, and numerous
sandbanks.   A little after six we anchored off a
district of Ibo villages, called Okoh, on the right
bank; a lake of water was seen at a little distance
before we came to anchor: the country is very open.
We had passed two villages on the left bank before
we came to anchor, for we steered on the right
bank.   The villages are Osutshi, and Akra Atani.

July 26 : Started this morning about half-past
seven o'clock, passed several groups of the people of
Okoh, their villages being scarcely visible from the
river, with the exception of a few fishing huts.   About
ten A.M., some rocks were seen on the left bank, and
the country began to present an undulating appearance.   Shortly after, a group of about five hundred
people burst into view in Onitsha market, on the left
bank, trafficking by the water-side, with a great
number of canoes; we steamed past them, as we were
desirous, if possible, of getting to Adamugu before
evening.   Onitsha is the last market-town belonging to
Aboh, on the left bank ; a little while after we came to
the Asaba market on the right side; they consider it
the same as Onitsha, but no trade was going on, and
about half-past two P.M. we unfortunately struck on
a bank between Walker and Long Islands; we came
suddenly upon it, having just sounded three fathoms,

when the bow struck in four feet water: and with all the efforts we could make the vessel could not be got afloat that evening. Mr. Richards took the boat and went to sound about Walker Island, and returned late in the evening.

July 27 : After breakfast, Mr. Richards went to take soundings again. At noon the ship was afloat, and at half-past one P.M. we got the steam up, weighed, and passed Ode creek on the left bank, where there were some canoes;—this place is said to belong to Aboh. At seven P.M. we anchored opposite a place where the situation of the village Utò was pointed out, but it was not visible from the river. The navigation of the river from Aboh to this place requires very great care in crossing from point to point, on account of many banks which stretch across the centre of the river, leaving the channel very close to the shore. It was on such a bank, slightly covered, that we struck after sounding three fathoms; many of them being visible to-day, we passed them more cautiously, by sending a boat a-head to find out the right channel: with this experience, we hope to be able to proceed more successfully during the remainder of our voyage. When the Expedition came out in 1841, either these banks had not accumulated, or they were completely under water as the river was much higher then, so that the vessels went over all.

July 28 : Weighed at six A.M., and in about an hour we came opposite the first village of conical huts on the left bank, called Ommodomo, "Children's Children;" it being the village of Adamugu given

by the Atta, or chief of Idda, to his daughter as the
inheritance of her children.   Mr. Richards told me
that Dasaba Nufi, king of Lade, brought his forces
down to this place when he contemplated attacking
the inhabitants of the Delta, to revenge the murder
of Mr. Carr.   I shall relate the particulars respecting Dasaba's expedition hereafter.   We commenced
speaking with the people here in Yoruba as well
as in Haussa, because there are Yoruba and Haussa
slaves in this neighbourhood.   About nine A.M. we
came opposite the town of Adamugu, where one
oblong and three round huts were seen near the
water-side, on the left bank; the town itself being a
little way inland.   From Onitsha market to Adamugu, the banks presented at times the appearance
of mud walls, about six feet high from the water's
edge.   The interior of the country now and then assumed an open appearance.   From Onitsha market to
Adamugu the country is very thinly populated, and
appears low and swampy in many places.   We were
steaming rapidly on, and every one was in hopes of
getting near Igára this evening, when, unfortunately,
we took a channel which had been blocked up, and
as we were returning to find another, the ship stuck
fast in one fathom water.   With all our efforts for
the whole afternoon, she could not be floated off.

July 29 : The labour of getting the ship afloat
was resumed, but without success till about four P.M.,
when she dropped down to the middle of the stream,
and lay there at anchor.   After dinner, a party of
us landed on the beach of a sandy island, abreast
of which we had grounded, to take a little exercise,

while the ship was dropping down. We rejoined her about seven P.M. The country is open, and the weather cool and pleasant; the nearest village below us is Ami-Doko, a few miles above Adamugu.

July 30: *Sunday.* As the men had laboured so very hard from Friday till late on Saturday, we remained quietly at anchor to-day, and had service at half-past ten. I preached from Matt. vii. 13. Several canoes came alongside, as on other days, to sell provision and cloths, but they were sent away, as it was the Lord's-day, in which we do no work. This they seem to understand as soon as they are told it, because Mr. Beecroft in his many voyages up this river told them the same.

July 31: Got under weigh this morning at half-past six. About nine we came abreast of Lander's Island, where the inhabitants of Oko Idoko and Abijaga, on the point of the first island, were seen on the bank, gazing at us as we passed. About five P.M. we anchored some little distance off Idda for convenience of wooding. Two messengers were immediately despatched to announce our arrival, and to tell them that we would pay the Atta an early visit the next morning. This precautionary step was taken to remove every shadow of excuse from the Atta, that it was contrary to custom to see strangers on the day of their arrival in his country.

August 1: I had already told the gentlemen to prepare for a hard day's work, for it causes more trouble to see the Atta than any other chief we have yet met with: accordingly, we partook of an early breakfast, and taking some lunch with us, started for

Idda about seven A.M.   On landing we saw nothing of our messengers, but proceeded to the town,
and there met one of the king's eunuchs, of whom
we made enquiry concerning them.   Without telling us directly where they were, he led us to the
house of Ehemodina, an elderly chief, and a relative
of the late Abokko, so favourably spoken of in
Lander's and Oldfield's journals, and to whom the
Landers were indebted for the preservation of their
lives in their exploration of the Niger.   Abokko's
family has ever since been considered, by right, the
agent through whom all white men must be introduced to the Atta.   In this place we met our messengers, who had been detained since last night, till
messengers should arrive from English Island, where
an army of about five hundred men were encamped, to encounter the party of one Agabidoko,
their opponents.   It was nearly noon before the
expected messengers arrived, and from the severe
rebuke one of them received from the chief, it
appears that he had delivered a wrong message.
Ehemodina then told us, that we could not see the
king before to-morrow.   We told him we could not
wait so long, as we were in a hurry to ascend the
river.   He said he was in a difficulty; for he did not
like us to go to the king without the consent of
Abokko's son, or else Abokko's name would be dis-
honoured.   He then asked whether we should like
to go to English Island and see Abokko's son
there, that he might send some one to take us to
the Atta, and promised himself to accompany us to
the river side.   To this we consented, as we had

determined to see the Atta to-day, and not be un-
necessarily detained, and accordingly, Ehemodina
ordered his old, but very poor white mare to be
saddled. As we kept him briskly engaged in conversation, he had no time to go in to dress himself
for the ride, so he called for his dresses, and put them
on where we were sitting, and started with us immediately. We had to retrace our steps nearly a
mile to the river's edge, where we embarked for
English Island, distant about two miles, to the
point where Okeyin, Abokko's son, was encamped
with about five hundred men. We were led to his
shed, and immediately commenced business. He
wished us to stay till to-morrow before seeing the
king; but we objected to this, and told him that we
had taken the trouble to come to him, and to give
him the honour due to him, that we might be able to
accomplish our object to-day. He thought it would
be proper that the ship should come near first,
before we saw the Atta. I told him that the ship
was taking in wood, and we came to do business
at the same time; besides this, it would make no
difference to the Atta whether the ship was near or
far; for when Captain Trotter brought four ships
here, thirteen years ago, and invited the Atta on
board, he refused to come, because, he said, "the
king never goes into a canoe."* After a pause, he
wished us to show him what we were going to give
the king. I told him it is not the white man's
fashion to show to others what he intends giving
to his friend, and applied the case to themselves,

* See Schön and Crowther's Journal, p. 86.

asking them, if I were going to give a needle to any
of them, whether it would be right to exhibit it to
everybody. I added, that we did not know what we
might be disposed to give to any person, until we
had proved him by the word of his mouth and his
conduct; and that if he deserved it, I might be
disposed to give him the jacket off my back. Here
they were put to silence. Otí, an intelligent-looking
man, was immediately called to accompany us to the
Atta, and Okeyin promised to get some eatables ready
for us against our return; so we started again for
the town, and took our lunch in the boat as we
went along. Immediately on landing, we met a band
of drummers and a fifer, who began to play; and
Otí, the messenger, gave us a dance, flinging his
sheathed sword in the air, which he caught with
precision, and shook it towards us to signify what
an expert man he was. This revived our party a
little, for they seemed somewhat weary in walking
up and down the hill of Idda from morning till
the afternoon, while nothing apparently had as yet
been effected. Otí led us again to the house of
Ehemodina, from which place we started for the
king's palace, nearly a mile further up the hill.
After many zigzag turnings, and passing many low
doorways and porches, which followed one another
in a manner too irregular to be described, we were
stopped at a small opening to await the Atta's
invitation. It would be superfluous to state the
inconvenience experienced from the closeness of the
place, increased by the assembled crowd. Mats were
at length produced, but the floor was so uneven

that sitting was as uncomfortable as standing. A pot of bamboo wine was sent in for our refreshment, but it was so sour that none of us could drink it, and it was given to the spectators, who enjoyed it much. A calabash of good cold water was brought, which was refreshing. We waited about an hour and a half, I need not say with much impatience, but with this consolation, that the business once over to-day, it would not be repeated to-morrow. At last we received the welcome message that we were called in by the Atta. We found him sitting outside the verandah of the palace, on a mud-bank overspread with cloth, with an old carpet at his feet; on the carpet were placed his royal message sticks, with brass bells attached to them; and an old broken Souter-johnny jug stood before him. He had on a silk velvet tobe, and a crown of white beads, fringed with red parrot-tails in the front, with other fanciful decorations. His neck was covered with a large quantity of strung cowries, and coral and other beads. It was the same Atta visited by Captain Trotter in 1841. After the usual custom of paying and receiving homage from his subjects, he asked the Europeans to shake hands with him, which they did; after which, I and Mr. Richards were asked to do the same; we then took our seats. He expressed his joy at seeing white men in his country again. We communicated with him through the medium of Haussa and Igára interpreters; Aliheli interpreted for us in Haussa, and one of the Atta's men, who spoke Haussa, repeated the words to him in the Igára language. Dr. Baikie

having instructed me what to say, because Aliheli
could understand me better, I commenced by reminding the Atta of the visit paid to this place thirteen
years ago by four ships, and told him that Captain
Trotter was still living ; that the Queen, who sent
Captain Trotter at that time, has now sent Dr. Baikie,
accompanied by Messrs. May and Dalton, to ask after
his welfare, and to see whether the country is at
peace, and the Atta as well disposed now as at that
time ; that the Queen has not forgotten him, nor the
treaties she had made with him through Captain Trotter. He replied, that he remembered Captain Trotter's
visit perfectly well, and that all things remained
just as they were at that time. He was reminded
that Captain Trotter had promised that traders would
be sent to deal with him. Dr. Hutchinson was then
introduced as a merchant who was come to trade
with him ; upon this he ordered his attendants to give
shouts of approbation, and expressed his great joy at
the news. He said the place which Captain Trotter
had selected for a trading establishment at the Confluence was not a suitable one, being too much out of
the way, and liable to be disturbed by the Filatas ;
and that he would rather advise the merchants to
establish themselves at Idda, or at Ikiri market, which
is so near that when a stranger was living there,
he would be able to send a messenger every morning to ask after his health, which he could not do if
he lived at the Confluence. I admitted the truth
of what he said, but told him to consider that white
men are very sensible, and always take right steps
to accomplish their objects. I asked if any per-

son were to be troubled with boils on his foot, whether it would alleviate the pain, to apply salve to
his head? He replied, No. I said,—Well, in order
to prevent future disturbance by the Filatas, the
Queen has sent some gentlemen to go by land from
the north to the Sokoto, Bornu, and Haussa countries, to make treaties of peace and commerce with
those nations, and to tell them, that not only they,
but all the countries on the banks of the Niger
and Tshadda, such as Ibo, Igára, and Nufi, are
their friends, and that they should not be disturbed.
To this they all gave shouts of approbation. He
was told that two of those gentlemen were in the
interior, and that the ship would start to-morrow to
meet them and take them on board. When the Atta
heard that the ship would start to-morrow he was
displeased, and said it must not go till some trade was
done here first. I then asked him how he thought
a man should act when he hears that his companion
is carrying a heavy load on his head, and is weary
of his journey? Would he say, let me first go to
the market and sell all my goods, before I go to meet
and help him? He said, No. I told him the case
of our friends in the interior was just so. He then
urged for five days stay, alleging that the water
has not yet covered all the rocks; and promised to
send some one to accompany us. He was told that
it was better for us to go higher up before the rocks
were covered, and that if we stay later, the water
will not wait five days for us when it begins to
subside. He at last pressed for to-morrow, as he had
something to trade with, and eventually six hours,

that is till noon, was promised for this purpose. I next reminded him of another subject Captain Trotter had brought before him, namely, whether he would allow his people to learn the white man's book, and to embrace their religion, as they teach it in other countries; telling him that I was particularly sent to ascertain his disposition in this respect. He said, he remembered the proposal, and was as willing as before. The presents were then given, and about half-past five P.M., as it threatened to rain, the Atta withdrew, and we returned to the water-side just before dark, much satisfied at having accomplished this most disagreeable task. The political state of Idda at this time, like other places, is becoming confused by divisions and party quarrels. This proves that the power of the Atta is waning, and he may not be able long to retain his authority over a great part of his subjects, if these party quarrels are not soon put an end to. Since the death of Abokko, so frequently mentioned by the Landers and Oldfield in their journals, the town of Idda has greatly suffered; a great portion of the population, chiefly Abokko's party, have left Idda, and parts of the town they used to occupy are overgrown with luxuriant grass, which gives the town a very deserted appearance. Those who left the town are residing all along the left bank, from Adamugu, a great way towards the Confluence, hence the number of villages which go by the name of Abokko, or some one or other of his children. It is said when the present quarrel is settled, Okeyin and his party will quit the town of Idda.

The present dispute, which caused Okeyin to encamp on English Island, is thus related:—Some quarrel originated at Asaba market near Onitsha, with one Agabidoko, whose father was an Igára by birth, but his mother an Ibo. Agabidoko's people, for some offence given, attacked Abokko's people in the market, when several of the latter were wounded and killed. By way of retaliation, Abokko's people seized a wife of Agabidoko, and kept her in custody at Idda. Aje undertook a journey of ninety-five miles from Aboh to settle the matter, but he could not obtain an interview with the Atta, though the path was cleared for him from the palace to the water-side. It would seem that as Abokko's people are the most powerful at Idda, the Atta was afraid to offend them, but whatever might be the reason, Aje had to return unsuccessful. A few days after Aje's return, Agabidoko's people made war against Abokko's people, but had a bloodless battle, the latter being on the island, and the former on the river, and on their departure they took five Idda canoes away with them from the water-side;—in this state the matter still remains. When we were waiting at Ehemodina's house, he expressed his wish that we should interfere in settling the matter between the two contending parties; and he was told that, if the Atta should seek advice from the commissioned officer, or request him to act as a peace-maker between them, he would have no objection to do so. But the king never said a single word on the subject, and even when particularly asked whether the town and country were at peace, he answered in the affirmative.

August 2 : As we could not call at English Island yesterday to report the result of our interview with the Atta, we sent the messenger to tell Okeyin that we would call on him when the ship came near in the morning. We anchored close to the town, at the point of the cliff, to land some coals and to trade with the people till noon. A great number of people soon came alongside, and the 'Pleiad' was full of them. I accompanied Dr. Baikie to English Island with some presents for Okeyin, Ehemodina, and Otí the messenger. In return, Okeyin gave the Doctor two goats, and about forty yams, and we returned on board. Two of the Atta's daughters came to see the ship; they were shown into the saloon, and something was given them to eat, but they were too bashful to partake of it. Otí took care to wrap it up carefully for them to take away; and they received presents from Drs. Hutchinson and Baikie, and I added two small glass plates, sent me by Lady Buxton, with which they were highly pleased. At half-past one P.M. we weighed, and steered very close to the cliff on which the town is situated, which presents a very romantic appearance, and is said to be about one hundred and fifty feet above the river. We proceeded about ten miles, and experienced some difficulty in finding the right channel; getting frequently into shoal water, from banks being a-head in various directions, in consequence of old channels being blocked up and new ones formed. Mr. Richards took the boat to sound, when the ship dropped anchor for the night.

August 3 : Got under weigh about six A.M.;

and after some difficulties, we at last found the right channel, and made a good progress, the river becoming more contracted, and consequently deeper. We anchored abreast of Soracte mountain for the night. The people showed some timidity at first, but by persuasion they came on board with some ivory. The left bank of the river is now more thickly populated than in 1841. In consequence of the invasions of the Filatas, all the inhabitants of the right side have removed to the left, and built their houses upon the mountains as places of refuge. The right bank is more easily accessible to those marauders, but they would have difficulty in crossing the river before they could gain access to the mountains, as their chief strength lies in their many horses with which they chase this poor and defenceless people. No one who beholds it can conceive how this mountainous country can be unhealthy; the wind was fresh and pleasant, and every one seemed to enjoy it much. Many rocks which were covered when we were here in September 1841, are several feet above water, which shows that we must yet expect a greater rise of the river than at present.

August 4 : Got under weigh as usual, but when not more than a mile from the Confluence, the 'Pleiad' struck on a bank immediately after sounding three fathoms, opposite the town of Igbégbe. While they were heaving her off, Dr. Baikie, Mr. May, Mr. Richards and myself, landed at the town, to see the chief and collect some information. We were led into the house of Ama-Abokko, the principal chief in this district. He is the eldest son of the late

Abokko of Idda, and brother of Okeyin, who was encamped on English Island. Ama-Abokko received us very kindly, and admitted us to the back piazza of his private apartment, where he seated us; and we told him the object of our visit to the Niger at this time. Ama-Abokko was not at this place when the Expedition was here in 1841, and the town was very small then; but since Dasaba's invasion of the right bank, a great many of the inhabitants of that part of the river have fled to this place, and to other localities on the left side, for security. The inhabitants of Mount Patteh were obliged to give up their stronghold, because Dasaba disturbed them for two years. Ama has not received any intelligence about the white men who are travelling in the interior. From him we learnt, for the first time, that Panda (Fundah of Laird) was destroyed by the Filatas only three months ago, that the king was killed, and that the Filatas were about Toto, for whose safety he expressed much doubt. At our request he promised to send some messengers with us to tell us the names of the villages and places on the banks of the Tshadda as we ascend; and we invited him on board the next morning. Here also was confirmed information which we had received at Adamugu, that Dasaba was driven out of Lade by his brother near Rabba, because the Nufi people preferred him to Dasaba, the latter being too tyrannical for them, and putting many people to death unmercifully for trifling offences. Dasaba has fled to Ilorin for refuge.

Mr. Richards, who accompanied Mr. Beecroft to

Rabba in his last visit to that place in 1845, informed me, that Dasaba had told them when at Lade, that his expedition towards the Delta, was to revenge the death of Mr. Carr; that king Obi of Aboh had sent to inform the Atta of Igára of the conduct of the inhabitants of the Delta, who had killed the white man coming to establish trade with the upper country, and that something must be done to keep the road open for free communication between them and the white men : that the Atta not having sufficient power to do this, sent to him as one concerned in the matter, and powerful enough to keep the road open; and that he promised to bring a large force of horse and foot, provided the Atta would furnish canoes to take them across the creeks and rivers. Accordingly Dasaba brought down a large force, and encamped for a considerable time at the model farm : the Kakandas joined his army, and they marched downwards as far as opposite Adamugu, when Dasaba commenced his attack seaward, at which time about one hundred towns and villages were destroyed, but being afraid of losing many of his men and horses in the swamps, he returned. But as they have no principle to restrain their cupidity in time of war, the remainder of the Kakandas who had not taken timely warning to flee for safety to the left bank out of the way, fell a prey to Dasaba's soldiers on their way home. Thus nearly all the right bank of the Niger, from opposite Adamugu to the Confluence, has scarcely a village to be seen, while the left bank is full of new and extensive towns and villages, which were not there in 1841. The very

mention of Dasaba's name is odious in the ears of
the natives about the Confluence.

August 5 : Started early this morning with Drs.
Baikie and Hutchinson, and Mr. May, to go to the
top of Mount Patteh.   Mr. May wished to sketch
from that elevation, of about twelve-hundred feet,
the juncture of the Kowara and Tshadda, but owing
to the desolated state of the country, the valley
was so overgrown with wood and high grass, as to be
impenetrable, except where we came upon the track
of elephants, now the undisturbed possessors of
these once thickly populated districts.   As we could
not go on because of the thick grass and swamps, we
returned to the boat and pulled further up, till we
came to a landing-place, where a small canoe was
seen under the trees, belonging to a small village of
eight or ten huts, a scanty remnant of the once
secure villages of Mount Patteh.   This village is
built on the first cone, about a third part of the
way up Mount Patteh, where very old persons
only were living.   We asked them the way to the
mount, but they told us there was no way thither
at this time, as Dasaba had driven or carried all
the inhabitants away.   The sight of these villages
was truly pitiable.   They pointed to the site of the
Model Farm below, which is now covered with trees
and grass, and asked if we were coming to rebuild
it.   I told them it might be taken up again in due
time.   They entertained us, according to their means,
with country beer and clean cool water, which they
fetched from the side of Mount Patteh.   We promised to give them some presents if any of them

would come on board, and returned to the ship about
ten A.M.

Ama-Abokko, the chief, had come early on board,
and Captain Taylor had been talking with him about
trading affairs till our return.   Dr. Baikie called him
into the saloon, and gave him some presents from
Government, with which he was much pleased.   We
tried to get him to forward letters to the coast for us
by way of Ilorin, Ijaye, Ibadan, and Abbeokuta, but
he made so many excuses, that I evidently saw he
was afraid to do it, though he did not like to say so,
for fear of committing himself, because people might
accuse him of sending a bad book or charm through
Ilorin, as Dasaba their common enemy has taken
refuge there ; and he did not sufficiently know us
and our footing on that part of the coast.   We
reminded him of the person he promised to send
with us, and told him also, that we would hire some
of his canoe men, if he would let us have some, to
which he consented, and raised our expectation as to
his readiness.   Ama-Abokko styled himself the king
of this part of the country, and I tried to ascertain
whether he was independent of the Atta, but could
receive no satisfactory reply to my question.   I dare
say he did not like to tell us.   That we might see more
of the town and collect information, we went after
twelve to Igbégbe, each one in a different direction,
except that Mr. Richards and myself went together.
Ivory was shown us as well as trona, (salt packed up
in grass bags from the coast,) horses, and two slaves.
I offered to purchase one of the owners herself, instead
of the slaves, but she shuddered at the idea.   I left

her to infer from that the propriety of dealing in
our fellow-men. Some slaves were in a canoe alongside the ship to-day. It is not to be wondered at,
that many slaves are seen about just at this time,
for many unfortunate persons who have suffered in
the war between Dasaba and his brother, and such
as have fallen a prey to the Filatas at the destruction of Panda, are now scattered about the country in
all directions by their captors. Fortunately, they
must remain in the country, as there is no place
known in the Bight of Biafra for exportation of
slaves, the only foreign slave-markets being Whydah
and Porto Novo, in the Bight of Benin.

From the town of Igbégbe is visible that of Patta,
about two miles distance. There are two places of
this name, the first, near the left bank of the Tshadda,
the other, between the first Patta and Tshewu. The
first Patta and Tshewu are at war with Igbégbe,
and soldiers come by stealth from them and shoot
people, or catch them at Igbégbe and run away. I
believe these two Pattas are inhabited by the people
of Mount Patteh, who have taken refuge on the
banks of the Tshadda. The chief, Ama-Abokko,
never mentioned the circumstance of there being
war between them, but always said there was peace.
We returned on board about sunset.

August 6: *Sunday.* Had service on board at
half-past ten: preached from 2 Tim. i. 7, on the
former part of the text: " God has not given us the
spirit of fear," and applied it to individual members
of Christ's Church, but I preached in much weakness; may the Spirit of God carry His word home

to the heart and consciences of those who heard it! The people here speak the Igbira language, and we had no one who could speak directly to them. Our communication was carried on, either through the medium of Yoruba or Nufi, or through the Haussa language, before it was interpreted to the chief in Igbira. As this mode of communicating is a very inconvenient one, I was afraid of making use of persons who have not the least idea of the spirit of what I intend to communicate; and to attempt to convey any notions of the Christian religion through such channels would, I feared, lead to misconception. There are but few traders and inhabitants who can speak Haussa, Yoruba, or Nufi : the people in general speak the Igbira language.

The people were told yesterday, that to-day would be Sunday, or our sacred day, in which we do no business. They did not, therefore, come for trade, but a few small canoes brought beer and some eatables, which were purchased by the Krumen.

CHAP. II.

August 7 : Having laid in a sufficient stock of
green wood, we got under weigh about eight A.M.,
under green wood steam. The channel was very
intricate :—after a long zigzag passage at the mouth
of the Tshadda we got into four and five fathoms
water, with very slow progress, and hardly made
eight miles direct from the Confluence, because the
steam could scarcely be kept up for an hour together,
and the anchor had then to be dropped while it was
got up again.

August 8 : About eight A.M. we weighed anchor,
but in about a quarter of an hour the steam failed,
and we were obliged to drop it again. It was impossible to accomplish our object at this rate, two
days having been wasted merely for want of proper
fuel to keep up the steam ; and if the Krumen were
sent on shore to cut wood again, it would be as green

as before. Dr. Baikie, therefore, myself, and Mr. Richards, landed at a small village called Atipo, a little way higher up, where we saw plenty of dry wood in the town; we told the natives to take it to the water-side, and returned to the ship to tell Captain Taylor of our discovery, and to know if he would purchase it. One of the iron canoes was soon paddled thither, and in about three hours she returned deeply laden with dry and substantial firewood, which we hoped would enable us to move onward in our voyage. Several enquiries were made to-day of Dr. Barth, but no news was heard of him. In the evening a canoe came alongside from Ama-Abokko with seven persons, two of them being headmen; one of the headmen, Zuri, spoke several languages, and was a native of a town on the bank of the Tshadda, which pays tribute to Panda, and also to Wukari. This man will, we hope, be of great use to us as we ascend the Tshadda. We had thought that Ama-Abokko was not faithful to his promise, but we were wrong; and his sending his own canoe to overtake us after two days' sail from the Confluence, against a strong current, corrected our erroneous surmises as to his sincerity, because he was not able to fulfil his promise at the moment we looked for it. The native chiefs always take more time to think and arrange their plans and settle their affairs than we are aware of. We are very thankful to have these men with us, speaking Igára, and Igbira, or Panda, they being natives of the banks of the Tshadda, and as Zuri can speak Haussa, we hope to be able to collect much information.

August 9 : Got under weigh about half-past eight A.M., and anchored abreast Little Harriet Island at six P.M., the steam having been kept up sharp and brisk under a mixture of dry and green wood. The Tshadda presents in appearance the same expansive sheet of water, as did the streams of the Kowara and Tshadda united, and contains a good depth of water, and has been of easy navigation hitherto. The cliff on the right bank of the river, on which the village Ogbá is situated, is covered with luxuriant jungle, called Frenchwood in Allen's chart of this river. The name of the inhabitants on both sides of the river is Igbira, to whom the land of Panda belongs. The Atta, many years back, sent one of his sons to reside at Panda, which was tributary to the king, and this son ultimately became its sovereign. The boundary of Panda, in other words, of the Igbira country, is between Oketta and Abatu, the latter being the first village belonging to the Bassa country near the river side. Here we began to meet recent traces of the Filata depredations; the inhabitants of Ogbá, on Frenchwood cliff, were obliged to take refuge on Harriet Island, on account of the Filatas, fearing lest, after the capture of Panda, they might attack them also.

August 10 : Started about eight A.M., and arrived at Yimaha, on the right side, about noon, where we dropped anchor to get wood. Here again the inhabitants have been obliged to quit their town, and to take refuge on the opposite island, where they have built temporary sheds to escape the depredations of the Filatas; who, not content with the destruction of Panda, and molestation of Toto,

covet the poor and defenceless inhabitants of Ogbá
and Yimaha in their avarice. We landed on the
newly inhabited island, in which there must have
been a thousand people. We were led to the quarter
of Ozineku, their chief, a very aged man, seventy
years old, if not more. We told him the object
of our visit, and made enquiry after Dr. Barth,
but no intelligence could be gained. Dr. Baikie
told the chief to send messengers on board, that
he might give him some presents. Leaving the
island, we landed on the right side at the town of
Yimaha, which was deserted three months ago. Here
we met a few men who were keeping a look out for
the enemy, and at the same time were occupied in the
process of dyeing their cloth blue ; an art, which is
professed by men in this part of the country instead
of women, as in the Yoruba country. Upon landing
we saw recent traces of the Filatas ; only last night,
a horseman and six foot soldiers were sent to see
if the inhabitants of Yimaha could be easily
taken away. The spies finding the town deserted,
went through it, even to the water's edge, where
they stopped some time — quite recent traces of
their horses being visible. One can better feel than
express in words the distressed state of these poor
people, who are continually harassed and hunted
by the Filatas, the greatest pests of this part of the
country. They will not work themselves, and those
who will they disturb and seek to enslave, eating
up at the same time the fruits of their industry.
The hunters of elephants and collectors of ivory,
are either killed in their attempt to defend their

country and families, or are prevented through fear
from going about their lawful occupation; and thus
not only is the country disturbed, but the European
markets are left unsupplied. The men led us to the
house of the chief, and told us that the gentlemen
of the former Expedition resided there. We pre-
sumed that Messrs. Lander, Laird, Oldfield, and Allen,
were meant, who were here in 1832—34. While wood
was being bought, some tusks were purchased also.
We weighed about half-past four, and anchored
above Potinkia (Potingia) creek for the night.

August 11: Got under weigh about half-past eight
A.M. Before noon we were in shallow water, and
grounded off a small village, called Kende, on the
left side, but the vessel was got off again after a little
exertion : a part of the engine, however, called the
donkey, was damaged, so that we could make no
further progress for the day. In the afternoon we
landed at Kende, where some of the few who escaped
seizure by the Filatas at Panda have taken refuge.
Here again is a picture of the misery these poor
people are doomed to go through ; for they live
destitute of every thing, having escaped with scarcely
any thing but their liberty, and that with difficulty.
The Filatas, whose aim is not so much to kill as to
seize and enslave, took Panda by treachery. They
professed friendship, and entered the town on that
pretence, and the king presented them with bullocks
and other necessaries ; but when a sufficient number
had got in, they commenced seizing the inhabitants,
and scarcely gave them time to make resistance.
Only the king, Oyigu, and a few persons about him

made any effort to repel them; but the king could not long stand against his enemies, and was killed in the attempt. A great number were caught, and very few were so fortunate as to escape. The neighbouring towns and villages were immediately deserted by the inhabitants, who took refuge on the left side of the river. Here we met with a son of the chief of Potinkia (Potingia), who remembered having seen the white men on their visit to this river many years ago. We find the usefulness of having Abokko's men with us; the people would not come near us, until these men had told them who we were, and assured them that they would not be hurt. They then took confidence and came on board.

August 12 : After breakfast I went to the beach with Dr. Baikie and Mr. May, to receive a lesson from the latter in taking observations. Captain Trotter was kind enough to send me a quadrant by the "Forerunner" for the purpose, and I hope it may be of use to me hereafter. In the afternoon we went to the village and distributed a few cowries among the poor inhabitants, who were very glad to receive them; a few yards of unbleached calico would have proved a great boon to them, if I had had any to distribute among them. Dr. Baikie amused the children by strewing some cowries, for which they scrambled.

August 13 : *Sunday*. Preached from 2 Tim. i. 7., the latter part of last week's text. May the Spirit of God apply the word to each and all our hearts.

August 14: Got under weigh after breakfast

There continues to be a good depth of water, though the channel is at times intricate. The villages which we passed to-day are called Iyanpe on the right side, and Irigi further inland, and others, not seen, are called Betikia and Lesebu. Three villages are known by the name of Oketta on the right side, but the inhabitants have taken refuge on an island opposite for fear of the Filatas. A little while afterwards we came opposite the neat village of Amaran, on the left side, situated on the east side of the foot of Mount Pleasant, very appropriately so named. The village of Amaran could not have been there when Mount Pleasant was named, or it would have been noticed. We anchored abreast of Bay Island for the night.

August 15 : This morning we spied a few natives in a small opening in the bush on the right side. They were armed with bows and arrows, in readiness to repel aggression. Ama-Abokko's messenger called to them, as they were within hearing, to persuade them to come off, but they would not; he said they were Bassa people, whom he called Kaferi—wicked archers, who had hired the Filatas to destroy Panda, and are, therefore, held in great hatred by the Igbira and Panda people, to whose king they were tributary. This marauding tribe have destroyed towns and villages in Panda, and even to the westward of Panda, beyond the confines of their own district, which lies to the eastward of Panda.

The Bassa language is very much like the Nupe, with some little variation and peculiarity, as may be seen in Mr. Koelle's " Polyglotta Africana." * The

* " Polyglotta Africana ; or, a comparative Vocabulary in

village of these Bassas, abreast Bay Island, on the right side, is called Abatu, but it is not visible from the river. Here is said to be the beginning of the Bassa country. Three or four miles from our anchorage brought us to the village of Abatsho, on the left side of the river; here we anchored, and invited the natives on board. Three chiefs came off, whom we found to be Irobo, Itshigbasa, and Allagaba—the two former were sons of the late old king of Panda, Abuha, who was visited by Mr. Laird;—Allagaba was the chief of Potinkia. They were all taking refuge here on account of the destruction of Panda. Abuha was succeeded by his brother, Adekke, who reigned thirteen years, when Oyigu, who was lately killed by the Filatas, became king. Irobo has now taken the headship of the village of Abatsho. Enquiry was made of Dr. Barth, but nothing was heard of him; but they told us that in all probability we might hear of him in Akpoko, a village near the river, in the country of Doma, where Haussa people come to trade from the interior. Presents were given to these poor chiefs who were very glad to receive them. I encouraged them to hope for better days, and said that though the Filatas, their near neighbours, prove to be their enemies, yet God will raise them kind friends and well wishers in white men from a far country. A Haussa woman, named Asatu, came on board, and was recognised by Mr. Richards as one of the traders who used to be employed by Mr.

more than one hundred distinct African Languages," by the Rev. S. W. Koelle, Missionary of the Church Missionary Society. London, 1854.

Beecroft, and who used to receive goods in large quantities at the Confluence, to sell for shea butter and ivory, when Mr. Beecroft ascended the river. She was very glad to see a steamer up the river again. Dr. Baikie gave her a looking-glass. We weighed from Abatsho, and anchored a few miles higher up.

August 16 : Got under weigh as soon as steam was up. The passage continued intricate ; we had nearly reached Oruko, when we fell into shoal water and were obliged to drop astern to clear out of it, and anchored till the channel could be found. Afterwards, several attempts were made to proceed, but without success. The Bassa people, who had been driven from their towns by the Filatas, have taken refuge on the island, and on the left side of the river. They were exceedingly timid, and no wonder the sight of so large a body as the steamer on their waters was enough to frighten them, as they have already been placed in continual fear by the Filatas, the enemies of all.

August 17 : After nine A.M., Captain Taylor, accompanied by Dr. Hutchinson, and Mr. Guthrie, the chief engineer, went to sound the river, and did not return till the evening. The captain declared it was impossible for the vessel to proceed further. On this Dr. Baikie, wishing to persevere in the attempt, took entire charge of the ship. It would have been a great pity not to have gone further, as we had come thus far, and were still eight or ten miles below Dagbo, the furthest point reached by Oldfield and Allen; so that the new

ground to be explored by this Expedition would only
commence from that place. The health of all in
the Expedition having been so mercifully preserved
hitherto, every one felt a desire to go onward as
far as practicable.

August 18 : Dr. Baikie having now charge of the
ship, ordered the steam to be got up, and about seven
A.M., we were under weigh, having sent Mr. Richards
previously to sound the channel. About ten A.M., we
passed the most intricate part of the river, opposite
the town Oruko, whose chief Adama, is said to be
king of all the Bassa country. He sent one of his sons
with a goat to Dr. Baikie for a present, and wished
the vessel to stop and trade with him ; but said that
he had only ten tusks of ivory to sell, the Filatas
having wasted all his property at the destruction of
the country. Dr. Baikie sent him a message to wait
till our return, when we hoped to pay him a visit,
and trade with him also. Some presents were sent to
him by his son, with the message, that he should
warn all his subjects never to molest any white man's
boat or canoe that may be passing up and down at
any time through his waters. This message was
necessary, because the Bassa people are much dreaded
by native traders, on account of their thievish pro-
pensities. About noon, we anchored off Dagbo, the
termination of Oldfield's and Allen's exploration in
1832—34, where we remained and wooded during
the evening. The old town, Dagbo, appears to
have been deserted, and the inhabitants have removed close to the river, to a piece of land nearly
surrounded by a creek, which affords them good

security against the ravages of the Filatas. Dagbo appears to be the beginning of the Doma district and language. The scattered groups of huts which form the village present more the appearance of farm-houses than anything else. A great extent of land has been cleared, and planted with Indian and Guinea corn for the people's sustenance. They are very poor, and consequently had nothing to trade with.

August 19 : Mr. Richards was sent early this morning to sound the channel, and as soon as steam was up, we got under weigh and followed. After much perseverance we cleared the intricate channels, and got into a fine sheet of deep water extending to a considerable distance, when we came again amongst groups of islands, which occasioned frequent shoals. We passed the villages of Egy and Igere, on the right side, Agatu on the left, and Joko, on an island. These people are called Kaferi, or " wicked archers," from their disturbance of the water passage. About four P.M., we anchored off Akpoko, a very small village in the valley of the Doma hills. The ship touched the ground several times, but was always got off by backing the engine, or by the men going aft and dancing her off. As soon as the ship came to anchor, Drs. Baikie and Hutchinson, Mr. Dalton and myself went on shore. The town is accessible through a fine open creek at the foot of the hills, though invisible from the anchorage. The people at first showed some timidity, having never seen white men before ; but when Zuri spoke the Igbira and Haussa languages to them, they became confident. Many of

the people understood Igbira as well as Haussa. On
landing, we were led into the chief's house, where we
stood outside for a few minutes, till he came and
invited us in. He was an old man of small stature,
but respectable appearance. He was dressed with a
decent country cloth around his waist, and wore a
country shirt of patchwork pattern, of blue and white,
cut in triangles, of native manufacture and work-
manship, except the fringe on the borders, which
was cut out of red woollen cloth of European manufacture. He had a red Turkey cap on his head.
Mats having been spread for us, after the usual
salutation and customary compliments from Zuri and
Mahamma, our interpreters, they delivered the message of Ama-Abokko and introduced us to the chief.
Dr. Baikie told him the object of our visit, and made
enquiry after Dr. Barth, of whom we expected to
hear news in this place. But no intelligence of any
European traveller has reached this country. Magaji, the chief, acknowledged that Doma is subject to
Bello of Sokoto; but, as governor of the water-side,
he would acknowledge no superior, and said that
every chief rules his own district, of which there are
many in Doma. He answered questions respecting
the government of the country with much reserve,
especially respecting the Filatas; which shows, I
think, that if it were possible, they would eagerly
throw off the Filatas' yoke. We wanted to know
the distance of Wukari, but received no satisfactory
reply.

No sooner was the subject of trade introduced,
than six tusks were immediately produced, and

Magaji was very anxious for the ship to wait till to-morrow, when he promised that plenty more should be brought. But as Dr. Baikie had determined to start early to-morrow, so much time having been already lost, they were requested to send on board what they had in hand. Nine or ten tusks were brought and purchased that evening. The chief is saluted by kneeling on the ground, the forehead is inclined, and two fingers of both hands are rubbed in the dust, and dust rubbed on the forehead several times. The people salute one another by embracing, the right hand of the one being stretched parallel with the left of the other as far as the shoulders, or with both arms occasionally. The religion of the place is Paganism, for there were some fetishes under the trees, in front of the chief's house. The village comprises no more than forty conical huts, including the granary; and yet it is fortified with a ditch about twelve feet deep, and mud walls. The gate is entered by a drawbridge of three poles laid across, and is rather dangerous for passengers.

August 20 : *Sunday.* Got under weigh at six A.M., the river much improved, there being fewer islands. Before ten, the vessel touched immediately after sounding the great depth of seven fathoms ; she was hove off by backing the engine, together with the exertions of the men walking aft and dancing. We anchored, and had service at half-past ten. From constant excitement in entering an unexplored country, and other causes, which occupied much of my time, I could not complete my sermon : I therefore read the first and second parts of the nineteenth

Homily on Prayer, the subject I had taken in hand for the week. The most disagreeable effect of sailing on Sunday is, that it keeps the Krumen continually at work, cutting and splitting wood for fuel from morning till evening, together with frequent touching in shoal water, when all hands must run aft to dance the ship afloat. This interferes much with the sacredness of the day. When I thought how mercifully we had been preserved since our entering the river, now five weeks, no European having been laid up for a week, I could not free my mind from the apprehension of our incurring God's displeasure by distrusting His providence, in thus desecrating His holy day, in order to accomplish our objects, how noble soever they might be. In the afternoon, we got under weigh and passed the villages of Otia on the right side, and Aghadumo on the left, and Ayati and Zuwo on the right. At the approach of the steamer, the inhabitants of Zuwo quitted their village, and no trace of human beings could be seen, except the goats and fowls which they had left behind them.

August 21 : Got under weigh about six A.M. After touching several times in shoal water, about two P.M. the ship ran aground ; but with much exertion she was got afloat and anchored for the night. The country appears very thinly populated hereabouts. If this appearance arose from the fear of building too near the banks, because the river overflows them every year, we should have seen, at least, landing places as we passed along, but there was a total absence of such. The villages actually seen were

very few, compared with those on the lower parts
of the Niger, or the Kowara branch. The country,
for the most part, is open, though at times wooded,
and occasionally clusters of fine lofty palm-trees
occur, which show, by the old branches or leaves
hanging down from the head of the trees, that the
natives do not trouble themselves to gather the nuts
for their use. Scarcely any trace of cultivation was
seen along the banks, to relieve the eye. In the
night we had a heavy shower of rain, accompanied
with thunder and lightning, which cooled the atmos-
phere, for the sun had been oppressively hot of late,
and the river had fallen considerably. We had had
no rain, till last night, since we left Idda three weeks
ago.

August 22 : Got under weigh about six A.M.,
and after many slight touchings and heaving off by
backing the engine, at 12 A.M. we ran into shoal
water, and grounded about a mile or so below the
village Ojogo, to which we had been looking forward
as a place to anchor at, and get wood for fuel. With
great efforts the ship was got afloat by half-past six
P.M., but could not clear the shoal that evening. It
was with much persuasion from Zuri, our interpreter,
that the natives were induced to come on board; two
or three canoes afterwards brought some wood and
fowls, which were purchased from them. Their
canoes are very small, and are propelled by large
long paddles, in a standing posture. We made enquiry of Dr. Barth, but obtained no intelligence.

August 23 : Early this morning the chief of
Ojogo sent messengers to enquire after our health

and to show us the channel; but as they had no idea of the draft of our ship, their offer was not accepted. While the steam was being got up, Mr. Richards was sent to sound the channel; and on his return about eight A.M., he brought the welcome tidings, that on his making enquiry, he was told that two white men were not far from this neighbourhood, in a town called Keana, about four days' journey to the northward. I need not mention that every one on board was much rejoiced by this intelligence. We got under weigh, and after much trouble, the ship cleared the shallow bank, where we had been actually locked in. In a short time afterwards we anchored off the village Ojogo, situated on the point of an island, on the right side, formed by a creek which separates it from the main land. We immediately sent messengers to inform the chief of our arrival, and that we would pay him a visit soon. On the return of the messengers, we made ready for the village, but a great many of the inhabitants, and especially the females and young persons, were terrified, and fled from the village into the bush among the palm-trees. The men were armed with bows and poisoned arrows, and some with long spears: the latter formed an escort to lead us from the beach to the village where we met the chief sitting almost alone, under a large tree, which afforded an agreeable shade, outside the group of huts which formed his residence. After salutation by shaking of hands, Dr. Baikie introduced the subject of our visit, and expressed his wish to send immediately to the white men, who, we heard, were at Keana. Our previous knowledge of the case gave no room to the chief to plead ignorance, and he promised at once to confer with his headmen, and let us know, when we had returned on board, about sending messengers. In the mean time we had the man on board who had informed Mr. Richards of the travellers being at Keana. He confirmed his statement, that they had arrived there one month before he left Keana, and that he had seen them eight days ago, and offered to go with the messengers if he were sent; he himself being a native of Keana, where his father is living, but his mother resides here at Ojogo. We gave him some presents, and held out hopes of his getting more if he would go with the messengers, and bring our friends down. The pictures of the four travellers were shown to him, from the frontispiece of Petermann's Atlas of Central Africa. He looked for awhile, and pointed to that of Dr. Barth, which he said was like him in countenance, but he missed his beard and whiskers, like those of Mr. Richardson; he pointed to the picture of Vogel as his companion. From these and other testimonies, we concluded that the information was likely to be true.*

As the chief's messenger was not forthcoming, we sent to him again in the evening, to express our disappointment. The messengers returned, and said, as he was the chief of the water side, he wanted to catch some fish first, to send to the chief of Keana, who was his superior, and who would be displeased

---

* It will be seen, however, from the sequel, that the informant was misunderstood.

if such a present were not sent to him. To-morrow morning, Dr. Baikie and myself intend to go on shore and to push the matter forward. In the night we had a heavy tornado and rain :—the river may now be expected to rise.

August 24 : Early this morning we went to visit Amishi, the chief, about sending the messengers to Keana without delay. We succeeded in putting aside the plan of catching and sending fish to the chief, by promising to supply the messengers with presents to him. That arrangements might be made for their immediate departure, some one or other of us would have started at once with the messengers, had horses been obtainable, and if our appearance in the intermediate towns would not have caused delay, instead of hastening the matter ; for native messengers can go without much notice, and can make a harder push than any of us can do. After breakfast, Amishi, otherwise called Ojogo, which is his public title, came on board, and was shown over the ship and into the saloon, at which he was struck with great wonder ; about noon, he returned on shore to despatch the messengers, who were waiting to go to Keana. After the bustle of sending the messengers away was over, I collected some words in the Doma language from Onuse, the chief's sister ; and in return for her services she received one of the glass saucers, which were kindly sent me by Lady Buxton, with which she thought she was amply remunerated.

August 25 : There is a tribe on the south bank called Mitshi. They have been represented all along

as a wild people and wicked archers, and are called
Kaferi, even by their heathen neighbours. They
came once to Ojogo to sell provisions, but the
chief would not allow them to visit him, because
they are so much addicted to theft. Early this
morning a messenger was sent to Ojogo, to inform
him of our intention to visit the Mitshis, and to
purchase from them yams and a bullock, as we have
been told they have plenty ;—to-day being the market-
day between them and the people here. The chief
appointed Onuse, his sister, to go and transact the
business for us ; but when she came on board and
found that we had made ready to go, she was afraid,
and returned immediately on shore in her own canoe,
paddled by females as well as males—for both are
equally good sailors. Thinking she would follow us,
we started for the Mitshi market, about one mile
distant below Ojogo, several Ojogo canoes having
already gone before us. On our approach, we heard
a great noise and clamour in the market, which is
held in canoes on the water-side, and when we came
near, all the Ojogo canoes had dispersed in different
directions, and everything was in great confusion :
some of the women were crying, for the Mitshis had
plundered their property, and a strong party had
armed themselves with bows and poisoned arrows to
oppose our landing. We were but a few yards from
them, but could not speak directly with them ; besides
which, there was such uproar and excitement, that it
was impossible to gain their attention. They at times
beckoned to us in defiance to land, and armed people
were stationed along the bank to oppose our doing so.

There was not a single weapon in our boat. Dr. Baikie held out some handkerchiefs as an inducement, but the very sight of them seemed to enrage them. At last, an old grey-bearded man, who seemed to be the chief, with great passion and significant motion of both hands wished us away. As there was no alternative, we returned to the ship, and then went to inform the Ojogo of the conduct of the Mitshis. He had just ordered a canoe, at the report of his sister, to call us back. He said, if the Mitshis, over whom he had no control, should do any mischief to our person or property, the blame would be laid to him. Then we were told that the Mitshis were cannibals, and that they devour the bodies of their enemies killed in war. But I am inclined to believe that this act of savageness is only practised in time of war, to terrify their enemies, and is not an habitual thing. When the Ijebus invaded Abbeokuta some years ago, and were defeated, some bodies of the Ijebu slain, were cut in pieces by the Egbas, and boiled in large pots, that the Ijebus might have the greater dread of the Egbas. Ikumi, the chief of Ijaye, performed a like barbarous act when one of his wives was put to death, either for revenge, or to terrify others from committing themselves in like manner. Before we leave the river, we may learn the certainty of the Mitshis being practically cannibals, or otherwise.

It appears from the information we could collect, that the Mitshis were originally slaves of the Filatas and other tribes in the Haussa country, and that they made their escape from their masters, and settled

on the south side of the river, where they have been
subsequently joined by a great number of runaway
slaves ; and have thus become formidable to their
neighbours. In this way they maintain their independence, and are always suspicious of strangers
going among them. They look wild but timid ;
carrying always their poisoned arrows about them,
which they are ready to discharge upon the least provocation. Their villages, which are independent of
each other, spread over a great part of the south side
of the Tshadda towards the Akpoto country. They
have a language of their own, and seem to acknowledge no superior above the headman of each village.
These villagers sometimes fall out among themselves,
or village against village, and shoot one another
with poisoned arrows. The fact of their possessing
a large number of cattle seems to favour the report
of their having been at one time connected with the
Filatas, as slaves, whose cattle they probably used
to tend ; and since they have gained their liberty,
they pursue the same occupation for their own
advantage. Their being prohibited from visiting the
ship may be the cause of provocation, which they
retaliated this morning in the market upon the
Ojogo traders.

From Idda to the Confluence, all the land on
the left side of the river, and from the Confluence
to this place, is called Akpoto land, and bears the
same name at Igara. The Igbiras, Bassas, Agatus, (a tribe of Doma) and also the Mitshis, who
are found in the immediate vicinity of the south
side of the Tshadda have all come from the north

side, either as refugees or settlers; and are not the original proprietors of that part of the country, as they themselves confess.   Even the Atta of Igara himself appears to be a settler or colonist in Akpoto land, as may be collected from the following tradition among the Igaras:—

As I was comparing Igara words with Yoruba, I asked Mahamma, Ama-Abokko's messenger, whether he could not give me some account of the similarity between some Igara words and phrases and those of the Yoruba—for the affinity appeared to be greater than between any other languages hereabouts.   Upon this he related the following tradition :—In old time, the king of Yoruba made a journey to Rabba, when he desired the Atta to look out for a suitable locality for his future settlement.   The Atta accordingly took a canoe and dropped down the river till he came to Idda, which was the original name of the town.   There he met the inhabitants who were called Akpoto, and their headman Igara, from whom he begged for a place to settle in, which was granted.   Atta returned, and reported his success to the king of Yoruba, who asked the Atta, if he thought he would be secure and nobody could trouble him.   The Atta answered, that he should be secure.   Hence, the Atta separated and formed a district for himself; and being more influential than the Akpotos, they gave him the precedence.   In course of time the language of the settlers gradually disappeared before that of the Akpotos; or rather the settlers appear to have adopted the latter as a medium of communication between them, and incorporated it with their own. The true meaning of Atta, is *father* or *patriarch*, but his right title as king is Onu, which is the same as Olu of Yoruba, and means king, or governor of a province.

August 26. Nothing of importance occurred during the day; the little wood the people had was purchased, and the Krumen were sent to cut more in the bush. The wants of this people are so few, that they are content to sit down the whole day smoking their pipes, instead of going to cut wood to sell, although they are very desirous of getting many things by begging.

August 27 : *Sunday.* Had service at half-past ten as usual, and read the third part of the nineteenth Homily on Prayer. Having been informed that the people were running away from the village of Ojogo, we went on shore after service to ascertain the cause and quiet their fears. During two previous nights, Dr. Baikie and Mr. May had been on shore to take lunar observations, and of course had lights with them. The bull's-eye lamp seems to have made them afraid. The chief was previously apprehensive of something when he saw Mr. May measuring the beach, and thought that he did this because the white men had it in mind to take his country from him. When we got on shore, we desired an interview with him. His heart was throbbing with fear ; but I tried to explain to him, how from ignorance of the depth of the river, our ship was grounded very near his village, where we remained a part of two days ; that Mr. May's measuring the beach was to ascertain the breadth of the river, and how much it has risen since we have been here : that their looking at the moon and stars in the night, was to ascertain how far we were from our country : that he himself must have taken notice that the moon does not remain stationary, but rises higher every day : so by looking at either the moon and stars, we also know how far we are from home : that God has commanded us to do good to all men, and never to do evil, for if we do them harm, God will not be pleased with us. With this explanation both he and his people appeared satisfied. I asked him, if there were any thing of which he wanted further explanation, as we were ready to give it ; he replied, that he had nothing more to ask, but for some red velvet, a stool, and a bason ; which we promised to consider when our friends should arrive from Keana. We asked permission to walk a little about the village, which he granted ; but in every part of the village, we met bows bent and poisoned arrows ready for action. In one house, we met with Akpama, the Mitshi market-master, who wished us away on Friday ; he tried to keep himself out of sight, but we shook hands with him, and asked the reason why he refused our visit to his town, seeing we were walking as friends in the town of Ojogo. He laid the blame upon his unruly young men. We then invited him to the ship on Monday, to be accompanied by Onuse, the chief's sister, and Osaba, our Keana informant. He promised to come, but wished to go home first and give his boys some beer, that they might restore the goods they had taken away from the people of

Ojogo ;—then, he said, we might send one person, with the king's sister, next market, but no white man was to come till the market after next. When we returned on board, two chiefs, higher up the river, Mahamma of Kondoko, and Jefulla of Akpa, sent messengers to enquire who we were, for they were afraid, and to see the ship, which they did, and returned to their chiefs with satisfactory answers.

August 29 : Akpama, the Mitshi market-master, did not fulfil the promise he gave yesterday, to come on board according to our invitation ; but Mr. May quietly landed, and went to the Mitshi village, where he met the Ojogo's sister and Akpama, who received him kindly, and he brought them both in his boat to the ship. Akpama was very reserved, and felt himself powerless on board the " Pleiad ;" his weapons were left in the boat, with his dirty and ragged shirt, and he had but a piece of cloth around his waist. He was kindly spoken to through the Haussa and Doma languages, the latter of which he understood ; and two pieces of waistcloth were soon passed around his loins, with which he was not a little pleased. Allusion to his wishing us away was a painful subject to him. He said, it was a by-gone matter which he did not wish to be repeated ; and promised to tell all his people of us, and to bring the chief of Wantele on board to-morrow. But he evidently did not feel at home in the ship, and in about a quarter of an hour, he left it with the chief's sister, I hope in better spirits. If feelings of confidence and friendship are left to arise gradually in the minds of the people, we shall soon come to a mutual understanding, but when there appears to be an impatient desire to visit distrustful natives, such as the Mitshis, suspicion and distrust are awakened on their part, and are not afterwards easily removed.

August 30—31 : Nothing of importance occurred. The people continued to collect wood, and we were all in expectation of the return of Zuri, our messenger, from Keana, or to hear from him; he had given us hopes of his return in six or eight days, and it was now the ninth since he left. The rising of the river is one cause for desiring his return with some anxiety, lest we should lose the most favourable season for going as high as possible before the river begins to fall. Our expectation of the arrival of the travellers is also another matter of great importance, and one which cannot be easily laid aside.

September 1 : Many enquiries have been made after Zuri. Sometimes it is reported that he has been seen at Keana, but has not yet had an interview with the king; at other times, he is said to have seen the king, but received no answer from him; but not a word has reached us of his seeing any white men at Keana. Aliheli was sent to one of the men who were reported to have seen Zuri, but he was told that the person had returned last night. All this led us to suspect there could be no truth in the information given us of the travellers. Zuri had left Orobo, one of his slaves on board, who spoke the Haussa and Doma languages, as well as Igbira, and his little son, Musa, continued under our care. When Orobo came on board, I questioned him closely respecting the intelligence about his

master, and finding he could not continue his lies
any longer, he said, it was the oracles which had
reported all that we had been told about his master.
That this was a mortifying business to us I need not
say. We went to the Ojogo, to express our disappointment, and to request him to send another
messenger, saying one of us would go with him to
Keana, to enquire after our friends. I proposed to
go on Monday, if Zuri did not arrive by Sunday;
but Dr. Baikie not wishing to lose any more time
offered to start on Saturday, and with this understanding we left the Ojogo. On our way back we
saw Osaba, who we understood had seen the white
men at Keana, only eight days before our arrival at
Ojogo. I closely cross-questioned him, when he
affirmed that he had seen them five days before
he left Keana, exchanging goods with the king to
the amount of twenty slaves, but that it was two
months since he had left Keana before our arrival.
This statement threw quite a new light upon the
subject. The mistake of eight days must have been
made by the interpreter in the multitude of questions
which succeeded one another; and we concluded
they could not have remained upwards of two
months in Keana without the news of it being
more extensively spread; moreover, had they been
there still, immediately on Zuri's arrival at Keana,
they would have written to acknowledge the re-
ceipt of Dr. Baikie's letter to Dr. Barth, by a
special messenger, if they could not have left immediately. The idea of going to Keana was, therefore,
given up, but two days were allowed for the return

of Zuri, and to complete our supply of wood; Monday
being fixed for our departure.

September 2: During our stay here, I have
managed to fill up the words selected for translation
into the Doma or Arago language, with a few additional sentences. My teachers were so unsteady, not
being accustomed to sit an hour together at such
an employment, that I could do but little at a time,
so as not to wear out their patience, and risk their
giving me wrong words. The hopes held out to them
of a little remuneration had considerable influence
upon them. I was very anxious to get a few Mitshi
words; but none of that people could be prevailed
on to come near us. Akpama, the market headman,
did not fulfil his promise to bring the chief of Wantele on board. Aliheli was sent with Ojogo's sister,
with some cloth to buy provisions and a bullock, of
which we heard they possessed plenty, but he could
get nothing. When he was bartering for a few yams,
some handkerchiefs he had to buy them with, were
stolen from him, and it was only owing to the kindness Akpama had received from the ship that
they were restored. Aliheli said they were about
him with their bows and arrows, as if they were
going to war; and, except Akpama, not one of
them ever came near our ship. Several strangers
from the interior, and from the villages up the river,
visited the ship and sold their little goods. Among
them was Asaba, a man from Rogan-Koto, one of
whose legs was bitten off by a crocodile, but the
wound has since been healed, and the poor man
hobbled from place to place with the help of a staff,

about four feet long. As soon as he was seen by
Drs. Hutchinson and Baikie, they began to think
whether something could not be done to assist the
poor man; and Mr. Guthrie, the head engineer,
contrived, and in a few hours completed a wooden
leg. Asaba had returned to his town, as Ojogo
informed us, to get something for presents to the
gentlemen who were making a foot for him; and
on his return, the wooden leg was put on by Mr.
Guthrie in the presence of many visitors, who were
not a little amused at the contrivance of the white
men. Our stay at Ojogo had its many advantages.
It has become known, far higher up the river, who
we are, and what are our objects, so that the minds
of the people are more prepared for the arrival of
the steamer.

September 3 : *Sunday.* I held Divine Service
at half-past ten, and preached from St. John xx. 29.
In the afternoon we went on shore to take leave of
the Ojogo, and to deliver him a letter for Dr. Barth,
in case of his arrival in our absence. The chief was
also presented with a red serge cloak, with which he
was much pleased. Orobo, Zuri's man, who understood the Djuku, or Korrofa language as well as
his master, hesitated to go with us, but after a little
persuasion he consented to do so; but said he would
not come on board till to-morrow morning. Further
light was thrown upon the character of Zuri by
Ojogo, who informed us that Zuri would not be
safe if he were to go to Rogan-Koto, in Doma, which
was his mother's town, his father belonging to
Abitsh, higher up in Kororofa. Both these towns

belong to Panda, their present inhabitants being permitted to occupy them for the convenience of trade. Zuri appeared to have committed himself at Rogan-Koto, and he was declared an outlaw, whom any one who met him might kill, so that he fled for safety down the river. We told the chief that we knew nothing of Zuri's matter with his people, but he was employed by us, and under our protection, and as long as he continued in our service nobody should touch him. It is very difficult to know with what characters one has to do. I had many times suspected that Zuri, while on board the steamer, was assuming an authority to which he had no right, over those who came to trade at Akpoko; all those who sold ivory had to pay him some cowries, as if on commission. On one occasion, a canoe paddled after us a considerable way, and passed us at night, not seeing us till the next morning, as we anchored in the open river and they went close to the bush. The hard bargain they made for their ivory, constantly going away, and coming back to see what they could get more, and their going away at last without selling it, led me very much to suspect that Zuri had a hand in the affair; but I may be wrong.

The chief town of this part of Doma is Keana, whose ruling king is Adaso, said to be an Haussa by birth, who pays an annual tribute of one hundred slaves to the sultan of Sokoto, through Bautshi. All the small towns dependent on Keana have to pay their share of tribute to Adaso. It appears from the statement of the people, that the inhabitants at

Keana sally out from time to time, and catch the villagers as slaves, either in default of paying their share of tribute, or for some other alleged offence. The people of Ojogo had to quit their old town, Ajamo, and take refuge on the island in which they are now scattered in detached villages, which all go by the name of Ojogo, their chief. Such tyranny may account for the hesitation, as to sending a messenger to Ojogo without some fish to conciliate the king's favour.

September 4: Got under weigh about seven A.M., on our exploration of the Tshadda and enquiry after Dr. Barth. The first village we came to, after leaving Ojogo, was Ajamo, where a canoe paddled towards us, to say they had received a message from Zuri last night, who said he would be back in three days' time, and requested us to wait for him, but not a word was said respecting the white men. I, therefore, considered the message to be a mere fabrication, especially as Orobo had refused to go up with us, and had enticed Musa, Zuri's son, to remain on shore with him. After breakfast we parted company with one of the canoes which Mr. Crawford and the second engineer were taking down to the Confluence of the Tshadda and Kowara, with cowries and goods for the convénience of trade : we parted with three hearty cheers. After passing several small villages, the first and second of which are named Kondoko and Amowo, on the right side of the river, we came to Rogan-Koto, situated on the slope of a rising ground facing the river, and walled on the back part. The

Haussa call it Rogan-Koto, but the people themselves call it Ajewon Igbira. We anchored here for
an hour, and went on shore on a visit to Sada, the
chief. The inhabitants of this place are Igbira, and
belong to Panda (Funda). They were permitted to
settle here in Doma for the convenience of trade.
Thus, they pay tribute to Panda, their lawful king,
and a kind of land-tax to the king of Keana, for
permission to settle in his territory. Here we met
Asaba, the one-legged man, who was very glad of
the leg Mr. Guthrie had made for him, and appears
to be quite another man since he put away his long
staff. He moved about the deck with much facility,
and could not express enough in words his gratitude
to his benefactor. One of his wives brought a
calabash full of clean rice as a present. The town
of Rogan-Koto has not been left unmolested. Last
year it was attacked by the Berebere, of Lafia,
and a great many of the people were carried away
as slaves. They have just returned to rebuild their
ruined houses, very few of which remain. To those
who had felt the distresses of war, the sound of
peace fell upon their ears, as refreshing rain upon
a thirsty land. They were kind, and wished us
many blessings from God upon the undertaking of
the white men to restore peace to mankind. They
had not heard any news respecting any white travellers. After leaving this place, we passed the villages
of Kondo and Akpa on the left side ; and about four
P.M., the town of Abitshi (Zuri's town), but we did
not anchor. It is a small but thickly populated place,
and walled around. Like Rogan-Koto, it belongs to

Panda, and pays tribute to him and Wukari, in whose territory the town is situated. The Wukari territory seems to commence about Kondoko and Akpa; but in consequence of the destruction of Panda, it is likely these places will fall into other hands. From Ojogo to Abitshi, the land rises and is hilly at times on the right bank. The river is very easy of navigation, owing to the rise of the water and absence of numerous islands. Indeed, we have not made such an easy progress since we left Aboh. The Mitshi country extends on to Wukari, at which place we expect to hear more of this singular people.

September 5 : Started early this morning from our anchorage, which was nearly abreast Mount Ethiope. The scenery is very picturesque, fresh mountains continually burst into view. There is plenty of water, and the navigation is easy. We passed several small farms and fishing villages, but as it was thought of more importance to push forward to Wukari, we did not stay to ask the names of the villages, though we had several of them given to us at Rogan-Koto. About two P.M., we came very close to a group of huts on the left bank, where it appeared they were making pottery, and dropping our anchor for a short time, we called a canoe alongside. The men told us that the name of the town to which they belonged, is Anyishi, a little way a-head of us on the left side of the river; and that they had sent to inform the chief that a ship was coming. The canoe-men hastened back, shouting, " Sariki n Wukari, Sariki n Wukari! (King of Wukari,

King of Wukari!) I judged from this exclama-
tion, either that the king of Wukari was there,
or that this place must be of some importance
belonging to him. We weighed, and in a short
time came in sight of the town of Anyishi, situated
on a hill on the west side of Mount Herbert;
but we did not stop, reserving our visit to these
places till our return. The face of the country
we passed to-day, was nearly like that of the group
of mountains between Idda and the Confluence of
the Tshadda and Kowara, but the hills are more
scattered, and present a beautiful appearance. At
times, the river flows at the foot of mountains
rising immediately from the water's-edge; for instance, Mount Herbert on the left, and Mount
Adams a little before on the right. The banks thus
present a very pleasing contrast to the low lands
we have passed through. From Ojogo to Anyishi we
met more frequently with villages near the river,
and the people were less timid. This, no doubt,
is owing to their having heard of the white men's
ship anchoring off Ojogo for some days. They
always showed a disposition to come off, if the
ship would but wait for them. The "Pleiad"
was well adapted for the navigation of the river,
and even when she went but half-speed, neither her
own boat, nor the canoes of the natives, though
well manned, could keep up with her in stemming
the current, which runs from one and a-half to
three knots per hour. We anchored for the night,
but remote from any human habitation.

September 6: Started very early this morning.

The state of the river continued very favourable,
the breadth not much diminished and good depth
of water. The face of the country is very flat
two or three miles inland on both sides, and there
was no appearance of town or village, nor even of a
fishing hut till about half-past one, P.M., when a
fishing hut was seen on the left bank, but nobody
was in it. At four o'clock we spied a group of
houses at a great distance before us. This was
something delightful, and about five P.M., we anchored off the villages of Gandiko, whose chief was
Ama, and Gankera, whose chief was Garike. Before
the ship came to an anchor, intelligence had reached
the chiefs of the villages, and all hands were up
in arms. Their weapons were bows and poisoned
arrows, and long spears, and some men carried three
or four of the latter poisoned also. Our boat was
ready for us, and we pulled towards shore in search
of the landing-place. There were some plantations
of maize and guinea corn along the water's edge,
and some of the farmers were near; three women
stood very close to the bank with seeming confidence.
We addressed them in Haussa, to which they replied, and asked them for the landing-place, but
they gave us no satisfactory reply. A little way
higher up, we saw a man on the bank, who drove
the women away. We addressed him in Haussa,
and he replied: we told him we were from the
white man's country, and wanted to see the chief.
As soon as he saw the Europeans, he cried out
lustily in Haussa: "*Bature Anasara maidukia na
gode Alla*,"—"White men, the Nazarenes, men of

property, I thank God !" many times over. He took
the lead through old cultivated grounds, but overgrown with grass and bushes, through which we
had to beat our way to the footpath leading to the
town. Our leader, either from excitement or in-
toxication, became louder and louder in his cry,
" *Bature Anasara maidukia na gode Alla !*" We
soon came to a juncture of two paths, where the
Galadima, a war chief of the first rank, and next to
the chief, with a small party of about twenty-four
men, armed with bows and arrows and spears, were
stationed, and our leader with his boisterous cry introduced us to them as men of peace and trade; in
the meantime, we were lost in the midst of the
soldiers, Dr. Baikie was in one direction, Dr. Hutchinson in another, and Mr. May in the midst of the
soldiers. We had not a single weapon about us,
offensive or defensive; but the confidence with which
we went among such an armed party was enough to
prevent their doing any mischief. During our whole
progress the few instances in which hostility was
shown or opposition made to our landing arose out
of nothing else but want. of mutual understanding.
On the present occasion, as soon as we came together, we shook hands with the Galadima, and he
led us to the town. The path was full of soldiers
coming out to join the Galadima; but seeing him
return with us, they all fell back on both sides of
the path which brought us to the entrance of the
town. The place was fortified with a wooden fence
and a ditch around it; and in the midst of the
town and under a kind of fig or banian tree planted

for the sake of its shade, we met the chief, Ama,
also armed with a bow and arrows as were about
two hundred men with him. We were introduced
to him by the Galadima, and after shaking hands,
conversed briefly with him respecting our visit to
the country. He appeared quite satisfied, and
requested us to return to the ship, and wait till
to-morrow before entering into particulars of the
object of our journey. We returned accordingly
with the hope that we might be able to visit Wukari
from this place.

What is generally related of the natives of Africa
as to their hostility to Europeans is not strictly
correct. The truth is, they take alarm, and consequently get ready for the defence of their country,
which is divided by wars, marauding and robbery
into many independent states, and every district
must watch against surprize by its neighbours. It is
but natural for such a people, shut out from communication with the civilized world, when they see
for the first time such a huge and self-moving
body as a steamer, to take alarm, not knowing the
object of those who inhabit it, for to their ideas
it is a town of itself. There is one thing which
enterprising European explorers overlook, I mean
the continual fear and insecurity the Natives are
in, from the constant treachery of their enemies.
This causes them to go about always armed with
their bows and arrows, and at the least alarm they
are ready to discharge their deadly weapons.
Though travellers fear nothing themselves, yet,
they should endeavour to take due precautions to

allay the fears of those whom they intend to visit, by previous communication, which will soon be circulated in the neighbourhood, and then all will be right. A prudent man will not consider an hour or two wasted to effect this purpose, rather than risk the painful result of misunderstandings which may never be remedied. As far as I know, there is no place in Africa uncontaminated with European slave dealers, which Europeans have visited with the intention of doing good, where such an event has not been hailed as the most auspicious in the annals of the country. Every chief considers himself highly honoured to have white men for his friends.—In the evening, the chief sent a vessel of beer and some eggs to Dr. Baikie for a present.

September 7 : About ten, A.M., we went on shore to have an interview with the chief. After standing about ten minutes in the front hall, which forms the entrance into his inner yard, he came out and seated us on a coarse mat platted of straw or small grass. After the usual salutation, we commenced stating the object of our visit. But Ama the chief was interrupted; Garike the chief of Gankera was outside, and he ought to have been invited in, which Ama did not feel inclined to do. A long discussion ensued between him and his people, and after a little cessation, Ama wished us to say what we wanted to say, and to give what we had for him, and then, he said, we might go and salute the other chief outside under the tree. He was answered, that we must leave it to him whether the matter was to be talked

over here in his hall or under the tree, for we were
strangers, and he was to give us directions. As we
would not proceed, he went out and invited Sariki
Garike in. This man looks older than Ama, and
neither of them appeared to understand, or at least
they would not speak Haussa, the Filani language
being their medium of communication, as well as the
Djuku, which is the language of Kororofa. Everything said in English was interpreted into Haussa,
and the Haussa was again into Filani or Djuku to
the chiefs. They had not heard of the Anasara
traveller, (Dr. Barth) and were very glad to hear
that trade would be established with them. They
said, if there was no trade with foreigners, the country would never prosper; that they were weary of
making war, to which they were always sent by their
masters, that they came to this place to settle and
cultivate the land, and that if they had anything
else to do, they would not go to war, unless for the
defence of their country, or at the command of their
superiors. They had heard previously from their
men, that we were not slave dealers, hence the turn
given to their intercourse with us. As regards our
journey to Wukari, after Ama and Garike had con-
ferred together, Ama replied, that they were at war
with Wukari, so that we could not go there from
this place. He asked whether we did not see the
town Anyishi on the hill as we passed up the river,
and on our replying in the affirmative, he said, that
was the place to ask the way to Wukari. After
Dr. Baikie had made them presents from Government, we obtained permission to walk about the

town; and visited Gankera, the next village, much
larger than Gandiko, where we saw some Arabian
horses in very good condition, kept purposely for
catching slaves. I saw two females in the town
whose only clothing consisted of a few leaves, and
who seemed quite unconcerned about their condition.
I hope to be able to learn particulars about this
people hereafter. We returned to the ship about
two P.M. While the Krumen were wooding, some
ivory was brought on board which was purchased.
A mallam, a native of Kano, who had come to this
place on a visit, told me that Ama had deceived
us as to the road to Wukari; and that had we
landed about three miles below, we might have
gone there, assuring us that he had lately come
from that place on a visit to the king, who gave
him the tobe he had on. There was another
Haussa man in Gankera, who was very anxious that
we should visit Wukari, and offered to place his
horses at our service, and to accompany us himself, but as Ama had put difficulties in our way, he
could do nothing. The pretended war, which Ama
said they had with Wukari, was of ancient date. It
appears, at one time, the king of Kororofa being
annoyed by the Mitshis, or some restless tribes
about him, hired the Filanis to assist him to conquer them. When this was done, the Filanis, according to their usual practice, settled permanently
in that part of the country they had encamped in,
and annoyed Kororofa itself instead of returning
to their own country; hence their war with Wukari,
and as they were too powerful to be dislodged by

the Djuku, and could not conquer Wukari, they became masters of that part of the country, which goes by the name of Zhibù, comprising six towns and villages on the left side of the river, viz. Hunue, Wazhiri, Gandiko, Gankera, Ibi, and Zhibù, the capital, higher up. Three other towns, Mitshi, Fagarike, and Baibai, are mentioned, but they seem to belong to Wukari. They appear, at present, to be at peace with Wukari, though the latter owes them a grudge for encroaching upon his territory. These marauders make yearly incursions into the Mitshi country, and the outskirts of Kororofa, and carry away captives, to sell towards Keana, in Doma, Bautshi, and Kano. The slaves are, undoubtedly, marched across the desert to supply the markets there, and this circumstance will explain the depopulated state of the country from Anyishi to the district of Zhibù—thus a distance of about forty miles, with beautiful ridges of highland rising beyond the magnificent Binue, presents a continued wilderness without inhabitants. In the afternoon the chief, Ama, came on board, and was shown round the ship, which surprised him not a little. The people possess a few miserable canoes made from parts of trees sewn together by ropes.

CHAP. III.

September 8 : Started this morning, and about
one P.M., anchored off the town of Zhibù. The
arrival of the ship at Gandiko had been heard of,
so that there was no cause of alarm, and we immediately sent a message to inform the sariki that
we would shortly pay him a visit.

The town is about a mile from the river, situated
on a rising ground, commanding a fine view of
the Binue and the country around, and appears
to be of greater extent than Idda in Igara, com-
pact and thickly populated. After about a quarter
of an hour's detention in the street, we were invited in by the sariki's messenger, and passing
three entrances of conical roofs, at some distance
one from the other, we came to a fourth, where
the king was sitting, ready to receive us. He told
us that his name is Bohari, but he is generally
known by the name of Zumbade, and is the head,
or king of the Zhibù district. He is by birth

a Djuku, or Kororofa, as are also Ama, of Gandiko, and Garike, of Gankera ; he seems to be about
forty years of age, and is rather of a surly countenance. After the usual salutation, Dr. Baikie told
him the objects of his visit ; namely, to enquire after
Dr. Barth, and to propose opening trade with them.
No intelligence of Dr. Barth had reached them ;
of trade they were highly delighted to hear, and
requested at once that the ship should proceed no
further ; but they were told that we must proceed
onward to make enquiry after the white man, if
possible, at least as far as Hamaruwa. The chief
said it would take us eight months to go there,
and the river would rise during this month only, and
begin to fall the next, and in a little time it would
not be deeper than a man's waist, so that our ship
being large, would not have water enough for the
voyage downwards ; besides which, there are many
rocks in the river, and he was afraid, if any thing
should happen to the ship, it would be attributed
to him, for not having given us proper information ;
that the people higher up were Kaferis, and would
run away when they saw the ship. We soon perceived his motives in all this, but thanked him for
the information. Dr. Baikie gave him presents
from government, for which he gave in return,
a sheep and a calabash of fresh butter, and an
Haussa tobe to Dr. Hutchinson. But there was
another question, which the most hardened con-
science must feel to be disgraceful to humanity.
The king called Aliheli, our interpreter, into the
inner yard, and showed him a little boy whom he

had to sell, and asked him whether he would not purchase him. Aliheli told him, that Englishmen were altogether opposed to the slave-trade, and when they came out, he requested that the ship might stay to-morrow, that his people might have the chance of selling ivory—a request which was at once complied with. We then returned to the ship. When the chief was asked if a bullock could be purchased, he said they had plenty, but they were with their masters. He was asked who these masters were, but gave an evasive answer; but we had learnt from the people that they were slaves of the Filanis, and came from Yola and Hamaruwa, which the chief did not wish to confess.

September 9 : While the Krumen were engaged cutting wood, the people came on board to trade. Bohari, the chief, rode close to the bank to see the ship, and to observe how his people behaved. With some persuasion he was got on board, but not before he had ordered all the traders to be removed from the ship. He, as all the others had been, was surprised at the size of the ship, and no wonder, for they themselves have but very few canoes, small and old, hollowed in parts out of two different trees, and sewn together with ropes, as one would join an old broken bowl. The ship's boats had to convey the traders to the ship, and land them the whole day. The kinds of grain grown here are maize, or Indian corn, guinea corn, and the straight-headed grain, called gero, and dawuro; rice is grown, but in very small quantity, though thousands of bushels of it might be produced yearly on the irrigated banks of this river, which would supply millions of people with wholesome food. In consequence of the men being chiefly occupied in marauding expeditions, the infirm male and female slaves are generally employed in the cultivation of the soil. No yams, plantains, bananas, coco's, oranges, cocoa-nuts, or pine-apples, are to be obtained—these plants not being cultivated. No eatables are hawked about the streets by girls and women, nor are there any places of refreshment, or eating houses under sheds ; in short, there is no market in this country like those met with on the west bank of the Niger. They barter one thing for another, corn for beer, and beer for corn, ground-nuts for rice, &c., but some people took cowries for ivory, to be carried to the Haussa country, where they are current. There is a total absence of palm-trees here, and consequently no palm-oil, and soap is a very scarce article. The people, with very few exceptions, are scantily clothed, ragged and dirty. Clothes are consequently in great request, so that in exchange for fowls, goats, sheep, ducks (of which they possess many), and for mats and corn, they ask cloth. The chief offered to send some persons with us to show us where the rocks were, and his offer was accepted, but they were not ready to come on board till the morning, and were told to be ready at cock-crowing.

September 10 : *Sunday.* Got under weigh at six A.M. The guides were not forthcoming, so that we went without them. About ten A.M., we anchored, and had divine service about a quarter to

eleven. I preached from Heb. vi. 19. At one o'clock
we got under weigh again, and anchored about
six P.M., having made about sixteen miles above
Zhibù. This morning, as the Krumen were set to
cut wood for the furnace, I could not but feel for
them, as they went very reluctantly to work. It
is a reproach to us, who profess to observe the
Lord's-day, and teach others to sanctify it, thus
to violate it ourselves. Six days hard labour is
sufficient for any man or beast, and all ought to
rest on the seventh. What good could I do among
the Krumen on the Lord's-day, when speaking to
them of the Christian Sabbath? No human habitation was visible from the water, and the country
continues low and flat; but rising ground, at times,
appeared at some distance from the river. A sin-
gular-looking isolated sugar-loaf hill was seen on the
left side of the river, in the direction of the back, or
south side of Zhibù. We anchored among a herd
of hippopotami, which were heard grunting about
the ship; Dr. Baikie and Mr. May landed in the
evening to take observations, but, from the proxim-
ity of these animals, were obliged to conclude their
operations as speedily as possible.

September 11 : Got under weigh about six A.M.
The country continued very flat for about three
miles on an average, on both sides of the river.
About eight A.M., a large forest of cabbage-palm,
or palmyra trees was seen on the right side of the
river, extending a considerable distance. The river
here spreads very much, and shows considerable
banks in the bed of the stream. In some parts

they are partially covered, and when the water falls
must form extensive plains of sand. We anchored
about six P.M., having made about twenty-five
miles. Flocks of wild ducks were sitting on the
sand-banks, but as it was getting late none could
be killed. A range of high mountains was seen at
a distance on the left side, named Albemarle Range.
No vestige of a habitation appeared all the way.

September 12 : Got under weigh as usual. The
country began to present an undulating appearance
at a little distance on both sides of the river. About
noon we passed a feeding stream on the left, the
first we have met since leaving the Confluence, and
immediately after, the Tshadda became extremely
narrow, being hemmed in by rising ground, especially on the right side, for about a quarter of a
mile. The depth was not less than five fathoms,
and the whole volume of the Binue having to pass
this narrow gorge, the current became so rapid,
that it was difficult for the " Pleiad," with the aid
of two small sails to stem it. We began to apprehend some difficulty of navigation ; but to our no
small joy, after rounding Lynslager Point, we found
the Tshadda spread its noble stream over as extensive a bed as before. However, being short of
fuel, we dropped anchor about two P.M., to cut
wood, but unfortunately, the trees hereabouts are
not of good quality, and only a little was cut to
eke out the scanty stock of dry wood on board.
A party who went shooting on shore, reported that
they had seen traces of human footsteps on the
beach.

September 13: We remained still at anchor. All hands employed in splitting the dry wood for use. A canoe with three men was seen this morning at some distance from us, but they immediately disappeared in the bush, and would not come near. We wished much to receive some information from them as to the distance we were from any habitable village, and from the port of Bomanda, which appears to lead to the town of Hamaruwa.

September 14: Weighed about 6 A.M., and about half-past eight we had heavy rains with a high wind, and were obliged to anchor until the storm was over. We weighed, and finding a large dry tree on the left bank, anchored near to it, about two, P.M. The men were immediately set to work, and some quantity was cut before dark. There is still no appearance of town or village, nor of fishing huts or traps, nor even of cultivation of any kind.

September 15: Continued wooding. About nine, A.M., three canoes were observed pulling downwards on the right side of the river. They saw us, and stopped to land their property on the opposite side, leaving one canoe there to take care of it while the others paddled across towards us. Every precaution was used to prevent their being frightened away. The interpreters accosted them in Haussa, to which they replied, and being invited on board, five of them came on deck. They were Filani traders in slaves from Bomanda, near the town of Hamaruwa. They left Bomanda on Tuesday, and made short journeys, first to Tshomo,

whence they went to Zhiru on Wednesday, and
then to Nak, where they slept last night, and
started this morning from Nak. They informed
us that we were in the Hamaruwa territory, and
that one day would bring us to Tshomo, the port
of Bomanda. They gave us the names of some
villages we should meet with on our way, viz.,
Nak and Zhiru on the left side, and Tshomo on
the right; and said, that the feeding stream we
passed on Tuesday is Akam river, with a village
called Wunubo on the bank of it; that there are
scattered farm villages in the interior, where the
slaves cultivate corn for their masters; that the
inhabitants of the Zhibù district are Hamaruwa's
slaves, and that all this country is inhabited by
Djuku or Kororofa, the same with Akpa or
Apa, which is the language of Wukari, the capital
of Kororofa, now subject to the Filanis. They
asked whether we wanted to purchase slaves, to
which we answered in the negative. One of them
said he had ivory at home, and he would be back
in two days, when he hoped to meet us and sell
it. They defined as well as they could the boundaries of Kororofa, Hamaruwa, Adamawa and
Bautshi; and said that the mountains visible before us, were Fumbina mountains, and that we
should be eight days going to the Confluence of
the Binue and Faro, pointing to the direction of
the rise of the latter on the left side of the former.
They added, however, that the people of Adamawa
were Kaferis, and that they were apprehensive
they would fight us. All this information was very

satisfactory, and we still entertained the hope of
being able to reach the Confluence of the Binue
and Faro. We gave them a few presents, and
showed them over the ship, which pleased and
surprised them much. They could give us no intelligence of Dr. Barth, nor did it appear that they
had heard of his visit to Yola. By six P.M., all
the wood was got on board, but the ship and
canoe were kept alongside the bank to enable
Mr. May to take a star's altitude. There were
some goats and sheep in the canoe where they
were always kept. It would seem that the scent
of these creatures attracted some wild beast of
prey, supposed to be a leopard, which approached
very close to the ship. A little before seven, as
Mr. May and Dr. Baikie were on shore taking
the observation, a growling was heard among the
long grass close by, and some of the sheep and
goats would have been carried away had not the
danger been known in time; or, what is worse,
the gentlemen might have been attacked when
engaged with their instruments. Several loaded
fowling pieces were fired off, which no doubt
frightened the beast away; but the period for the
observation was unfortunately missed.

September 16 : Got under weigh about 6 A.M.
The river keeps it breadth, but there is plenty of
water, from three to four fathoms. We missed the
channel, and the ship grounded three times, but
she was got off by backing the engine with little
effort on the part of the men. A new range of
hills showed itself at a great distance on the left

side of the river, consisting of many lofty conical
mountains.   It lay behind a long ridge of high
lands, running to a considerable distance, almost
parallel with the river, which presented a very
picturesque appearance.   The tops of some of these
mountains are covered with luxuriant woods and
jungles, and others are quite bare and rocky.
Though all these are pleasant to the eye, yet there
exists no trace of any part of them being inhabited.

About eleven A.M., we passed a small group of
huts on an island on the left side, which we supposed to be the village Nak, of which we were
told by our informants yesterday.   Our progress
was very slow to-day, both from touching so many
times when we missed the channel, and for want
of proper fuel to keep up regular steam; in consequence of which we were obliged to anchor many
times to get it up.   We came to anchor about six,
P.M., having made about twelve or eighteen miles
against a very strong current with a short supply
of steam.

September 17: *Sunday.*   Dr. Baikie proposed
to have service earlier, about nine A.M., instead of
half-past ten, and to make half a day's sail, and
meanwhile the Krumen were set to split wood for
fuel.   Accordingly, I performed service at nine
A.M., and preached from Dan. iv. 39.   There not
being a sufficient supply of wood, we could not
start, but the Krumen were kept at work splitting
till the evening.

September 18: Weighed about six A.M.   At nine
we saw the huge carcase of an hippopotamus floating

down the river, and about four P.M., we anchored
off Zhiru. The natives, who stood on the bank,
within hearing, and armed with spears, were at
first timid; but a little conversation with them
in Haussa, and a request to be supplied with provisions soon inspired confidence. We landed on the
bank, and shook hands with them, had a little
conversation, and made some hasty enquiries. They
were sent to inform their chief that we were
coming to visit him shortly; and a little while
after, the messengers returned to invite us to the
town. On our way to the chief, under the guidance
of one of the men, another motioned us back, and
introduced us to a Filani mallam, whose name was
Imoru, stationed here by Mohamma, the king of
Hamaruwa, as a kind of deputy or consul to watch
the interest of his king, because the inhabitants rob
and plunder travellers on their way to and from
Sokoto, Kano, Katshina, and Bautshi, as they carry
on trade through Hamaruwa to Adamawa. Dr.
Baikie being, for the first time, too ill to go on
shore to communicate with the chief, deputed Mr.
May to act for him. Made our usual enquiry after
Dr. Barth, but no intelligence of him was received.
Imoru confirmed the statement that the people of
Zhibù were their slaves. He was ready to send
a messenger to inform the king of Hamaruwa of
our arrival. The messenger, we were told, would
arrive that evening and return to-morrow morning.
Imoru could not give us any information of places
beyond Hamaruwa, other than the name of a town
he called Batshama, whose inhabitants he termed

Kaferis, and said they were a bad people. He asserted that it would take us twenty days canoe-
voyage to reach the Confluence of the Binue and
Faro, and that it is ten day's journey to Adamawa.
From this I understood Adamawa to be the name
given by them to a principal town in that extensive country. Hamaruwa and Yola are entirely
independent of one another, each holding direct
communication with the Sultan of Sokoto. The
present we brought for the chief was given to
Imoru ; but I suspected there was another, but
oppressed chief, in the town, to whom I imagined
we were being led when called back ; so I asked
Imoru to direct us to whom we should pay our
respect next to himself. He then told his servant
to accompany us in the boat to the other end of
the village, where we landed, and were conducted
to Fadon, the original chief of the place, and the
true patriarch of his people, but whom we met
greatly dejected, evidently oppressed by the followers of the false prophet. We asked after his welfare, and spoke kindly with him, but as he did not
understand Haussa, the servant of Imoru interpreted for him in Djuku, which is the language
of the inhabitants. A promise was made to him
that he should receive presents similar to those
given to Imoru, as we were not aware there were
two ruling chiefs in the town, and he was instructed
to send some trustworthy person with us to the
ship to receive them.

Since leaving Fernando Po, I have not met with
any people so much degraded as these. It is true,

that we have all along found the natives, except
the children, more or less clothed, but here I was
surprised to find elderly women with only a few
leaves suspended from a string round their waists,
with pipes in their mouths, and exhibiting the
greatest unconcern. This is the same race of people I saw at Gandiko, and at first, I suspected
they were Filani slaves, but upon enquiry, I was
told they were free persons. It appears that these
aged people would not change even the most uncivilized of their habits, though after their country
had fallen into the hands of the Filanis, the men
and other women adopted a better mode of clothing.

September 19 : There was nothing to be procured here, neither sheep, goats, fowls, nor even
wood; we, therefore, returned to the ship. Dr.
Baikie requested the mallam to inform Mohamma,
the king of Hamaruwa, that we would call on him
on our way back in a few days. The mallam
came to see the ship, and we managed to get
some more information from him, and then got
under weigh, in hopes of being able to find some
trees suitable for fuel at Tshomo, the next village, where we were told we should get plenty.
The steam could hardly be kept up, and we were,
consequently, obliged to drop anchor several times,
the current running upwards of three knots against
us ; but about four o'clock we were pushed forward
by a tornado from the eastward. The river takes a
northerly direction about this place, and we. saw
two villages at the back of the swamp, and the

town of Hamaruwa was visible from the mast-
head, on a hill at the foot of the chain of Muri
mountains. At six, we came to an anchor, in
hopes of getting some fuel, the quantity on board
being scarcely sufficient to get up steam. We had
made about eleven miles from Zhiru.

September 20: The boat was early sent on
shore to see what wood could be obtained, but nothing was found suitable to our purpose, the trees
being all green and sappy, and standing in swamps,
where the men could not have maintained their
footing, had the trees been such as we wanted.
Another boat was sent higher up, to see if there
was a village near, but it returned without finding
one. As there was no alternative, a look out was
kept to capture the trees floating down the stream ;
and two were secured before breakfast, the chase
affording us no little amusement. About ten another
was chased and captured, so large that it pulled
the boat a considerable way down the river, but
it was secured, and greatly added to our little
stock to enable us to get to Tshomo. In the
meantime, Imoru, the mallam of Zhiru, came on
board with the leg of a buffalo, killed last night
for a present to Dr. Baikie. The doctor would have
bought the head, but the superstition of the people
was so strong against selling it, that they begged
him not to be vexed at their denying him that request, nor could they be persuaded to sell the skulls
of hippopotami, which were piled up before the fetish,
in the town of Zhiru. I asked the mallam whether the people are willing to embrace Mohamedan-

ism ? he said they were not. Imoru very earnestly told Aliheli to ask me if I would pray for his wives, as they had no children. I at once called for my Bible, and read Psalm cxxvii., which I tried to explain to him, and showed him my arms and neck, to prove that we never used charms for any purpose ; telling him that we resign all our affairs to the hand of God, who knows better what is good for us. He was quite satisfied with my explanation, though he felt disappointed of his hopes. Imoru told us, that we should meet the king's messenger near Tshomo.

September 21 : Having succeeded in securing enough floating trees and drift wood to get up steam, we started this morning, and about noon several villages were seen at some distance on both sides of the river, which were Bomanda on the right, and Little Tshomo on the left side of the river : all situated on the plain, but sufficiently elevated to insure their not being flooded at the rising of the Binue, which is very considerable. Opposite Little Tshomo, we saw five men on a tree in the swamp, who had been stationed there to invite us to anchor ; the canoe which brought them there had returned to inform the chief of our approach. A little further on we saw a large number of people on the roofs of their houses to look at the steamer, while others waited at the landing-place to invite us to anchor, but as there was no wood to be obtained there, and we were told that at Great Tshomo we should get abundance, we did not wait. In a short time several canoes began making towards us, and as we had to anchor every now and then to get up the steam, they soon came up to us, and after a little persuasion came alongside. The principal persons were the brother of the late king of Hamaruwa, a son of the late king, and Ibrahim, entitled, Sariki n Haussa, an intelligent Filani of Kano, who was master of the Haussa language, and the king's messenger. He appears to be the chief trader of the king of Hamaruwa. In a little time they were at home in the ship, and became familiar friends. But a laughable scene of fear and confusion soon took place; the steam was up, and the vessel weighed; no sooner had the fan began to play, than the canoe-men, one after the other leaped overboard, and swam to their canoes in great consternation; it was with much persuasion that I kept the king's brother from following their example. The engine was stopped, and those who wished it, left the ship. Those who felt more confidence remained with Ibrahim and the king's brother till the afternoon, when we were short of fuel again, and were obliged to anchor about two miles below Tshomo. The report of the ship had reached the king the evening we anchored off Zhiru, and Ibrahim was despatched by him the next morning to wait our arrival off Tshomo, and to ascertain who we were, and what our objects, as well as to express his wish to see two messengers from the king of the ship to substantiate the report which had reached him, respecting the Anasara's ship on his waters. Ibrahim said, moreover, that the king would accompany the messengers to see the ship himself. But as we had not got to Tshomo, and there was no appearance of wood on either side of the river, Dr. Baikie could give no positive answer, but sent the messenger on shore to wait till to-morrow.

September 22 : The heavy pieces of wood which remained on board were split, and some empty casks, not much wanted, were broken up to get up steam. About breakfast, Ibrahim and the king's eldest son were again on board, and repeated their request for two messengers to accompany him to Hamaruwa, according to the wishes of the king. As I am not yet master of the Haussa language, the only thing we could do, was to take Aliheli as interpreter, and Mr. Richards and myself offered to go with him to the king. This met the Doctor's wishes, and about ten A.M., we left the ship in the gig, with Ibrahim, with instructions · to send the boat back as soon as we landed, which we supposed would be immediately at the village of Tshomo. A mile and a half from the ship brought us to Gurowa, called the king's farm, on the right bank, built on a small elevation beyond the rising of the water. Ibrahim landed here, and brought something with him into the boat; the Filani chief also, Shiroma Bukari, came on board to salute us, and returned on shore. This village is inhabited by the king's slaves to cultivate corn, and kill hippopotami, buffaloes, &c., for the use of their master. Two miles more brought us to Tshomo, situated on the same side of the river, on two small

eminences separated by a small creek, but inhabited
chiefly by the original natives, many of the females
being as destitute of clothing as those of Zhiru.
The mothers were seen carrying children in their
arms, or on their backs, with the hands of the
infants beneath their arms, by which they were
held fast. Here again I was struck with wonder,
at the low and degraded state of the human race,
when removed from all civilization. I asked Ibrahim, why they had no clothes, and he said, it was
their fashion. I asked for the chief, and he pointed
out an elderly grey-bearded man, standing under
a tree near the water-side, with only a small piece
of dirty cloth round his waist—this was the Sariki
of Tshomo. Before Ibrahim left the town, he managed to squeeze a large calabash full of Indian corn,
and some quantity of stinking hippopotamus flesh
from them, because they did not provide for him
when he passed the night in that village. I had
always considered the natives of Fernando Po to
be the most uncivilized I have seen, but this people
is more degraded than even the Bubis of that
Island.

The creek which divides Tshomo had not enough
water for our boat, so we had to pull through the
flooded corn fields to get into the main creek, but
as the whole was overgrown with grass and corn
stocks, Ibrahim was obliged to get one of the
canoe-men to take the lead. Our Krumen did
not like either the appearance of our guide, or the
passage he was leading us through. As a fisher
and hunter of hippopotami, he had with him five or

six harpoons or spears, and pulled through the
grass with his narrow canoe like a snake, while
the grass was so thick that we could not see him
ahead of us, nor perceive the track of his canoe.
However, we followed in his direction, till we met
him under a tree where he waited for us. We
had here to stoop beneath the low branches, but
a short distance brought us to the main creek.
The bank being only partially covered with water,
the men jumped out and dragged the boat across,
and our pilot then left us to ourselves. I called
the attention of Friday, the head Kruman, to mark
the direction of the tree, that they might not miss
the way on their return, but captain Friday and
his crew did not seem to relish the idea of returning alone among this rude and apparently fero-
cious people. We followed the creek, thinking
we should soon come to the landing-place, but
contrary to our expectation, we did not land till
one o'clock P.M., four hours after leaving the ship,
our progress having been down with the stream
since we came into the creek, which runs parallel
with the river. From all the enquiries we had
made, Hamaruwa did not appear to be more than
six or seven miles from the river; and considering
the distance we had made down the creek, I
thought we must have been at least three or four
miles nearer than if we had landed immediately
on the bank of the main river. It seemed to me
that if the Krumen had to return with the boat
against the stream, in the circuitous creek, they
would not get to the ship before dark; and under

the impression that an hour or an hour and a half at least would bring us to Hamaruwa, and that we might be back by five, and return to the ship together, especially as there was no other conveyance for us except two miserable patched canoes, used to fetch corn from the plantations; I ordered the boat to be pulled up, and leaving it and all belonging to it to the care of the headman of the village of Wuzu, we started for Hamaruwa.   An hour's walk brought us in sight of the first farm village, which I at first took to be the capital or its suburbs, but I was mistaken, and was told the town was yet before us.   Another hour brought us to a second farm village, and our way led almost direct west towards the furthest mountains we had left westward.   By the time we had travelled three hours, the Krumen who were as much deceived as ourselves, became very much dissatisfied, and they expressed regret that they had not returned to the ship, instead of going such an unpleasant journey in which they had no interest. Truly it was unpleasant, inasmuch as we were deceived as regards the distance, and the road was by no means enviable to walk in.   We had not left Wuzu half an hour before I was obliged to take off my shoes, and roll up the legs of my trousers to my knees, as did Mr. Richards, to wade through the continued splash of water and mud we met with more than one-third the way.   I kept pace with Ibrahim in hopes of sighting the town so as to convey the intelligence to my weary companions for their encouragement, but we saw nothing up to about four o'clock, when we came under a tree which was a resting place. I stopped Ibrahim, to wait for the Krumen and Mr. Richards, who were yet a great way behind, when Ibrahim to encourage me, said, we had made a little more than half way. While we were waiting, he performed his devotion. I told my servant to climb up the tree, and hail the interpreter, which he did for a long while, when Mr. Richards answered at a distance, that they were coming. He was obliged to beg water for the Krumen at one of the villages, for they were hungry, having missed their midday meal; and they felt it much, as well as the fatigue of a journey for which they were unprepared, to an unknown place among a strange people, who were only known to them as slave hunters through the country. Mr. Richards told me that he had hard work to persuade them onward. I encouraged them by reminding them that we were all similarly situated, but felt sorry for them as they might have got back, and thus avoided all this trouble. It was sunset before we entered the town of Hamaruwa, and calculating from the halts we made, and the great difficulty of walking in water and mud one-third of the way, that we did not travel more than two miles and a half per hour from Wuzu; we must have gone twelve miles and a half in a westerly direction before reaching the place. When we got half way into the town, Ibrahim showed us the king's house, into which he went, giving his companion directions to lead us to his own, at the other end of the town, where we were lodged. It took us about twenty minutes to walk to it; and all our party were glad to rest themselves, hungry and fatigued with so long a journey. About eight o'clock P.M., the king sent eight bowls of provision for us, enough for thirty persons, we being but eleven in all; but the Krumen, though hungry, did not like the Filani food, called tuo, made from Indian or guinea corn, in substance like hard dumpling, over which sauce was poured, and which is eaten with the fingers.* One of the men would not eat at all, so I gave him some biscuits we had brought for lunch, but had not touched on the way. Ibrahim sent two more bowls of tuo in addition to the king's supply, besides some nice mixture of fura, prepared from Indian or guinea corn, to be mixed in water for a nice cooling drink, with sometimes a little pepper and honey added to make it more pleasant. The king sent five sheep and lambs, with a kid, six in all, and a large pot of plum honey for our entertainment;

---

* The following description of the Yoruba method of eating their food is taken from Miss Tucker's Abbeokuta, p. 26, and will illustrate this passage:—The repast " consists of balls of Indian corn, called ' dengè,' served up in a kind of strong sauce made of beef, mutton, fish, or fowl, with various vegetables, and seasoned with salt procured from the Popos, and with Cayenne pepper, which grows in the country. * * * When about to partake of the food, a large earthen bowl is placed on the ground, containing the dengè and the sauce ; and the party sit down round it. The balls of Indian corn are taken out of the bowl, broken and distributed to the different persons, each of whom dips his portion into the sauce as he eats it. There is a good deal of animal food consumed in this way, but it is never eaten solid." From p. 117 it appears that the sauce of Hamaruwa is made with cow butter.

but unfortunately, before the honey was delivered, the pot broke, and the whole was spilled in the yard, to the great grief of all present. Ibrahim came with much sorrow to tell me of this great misfortune, and I must say, I felt the loss myself, because it would have been a very acceptable present to all the ship's company, considering that since the fourth instant we had been out of sugar. Butter and milk had been all consumed long before, and a pot of honey would have been an invaluable substitute. But travellers must take things as they come, and be content with such things as they have. The Filanis use no lamps in their houses in the evening, we had therefore to remain outside the house where we were lodged, seated in the dark, as they themselves did, till bed time, when a few sticks were kindled which gave out much smoke and little light, to enable us to ascertain the position of our bed, which was rough enough. Before we turned in, Ibrahim requested me to take care of my sheep and goat in our room, for fear of the wolves with which the country abounds. I told him it was impossible to admit five sheep and a goat into a room already filled with eleven occupants, and he promised to take care of them for us till the morning. Ibrahim's yard was full of visitors going and coming, to whom he was relating the wonderful news of the Anasara's ship made of iron, and moved by fire. Being tired with our journey, we left them to enjoy the story, and rested ourselves after we had offered a prayer of thanksgiving to God for his protection.

September 23 : I intended to pay an early visit to the king, and deliver my message, but he determined upon our drinking water first, that is taking breakfast before we commenced business; in the mean time he would summon all his head chiefs to hear the message from the king of the ship. About eight A.M., breakfast was brought in as last night, but the Krumen could not eat it. However, Aliheli succeeded in begging some cassada for them, which they greedily devoured. I was sorry that we were so situated as regards provision on account of the Krumen, and there was no rice to be had, which is their proper food; I therefore opened a small tin of sardines we took with us yesterday for our lunch, and gave it to them with the remaining biscuits to make the best of it they could. At ten A.M., a message came from the king that he was ready to see me. Without loss of time, we soon marched with a large party of Filanis to the king's palace; and after having waited a short time under a tree in the street, while our arrival was announced, we were invited in. Large curtains of country cloth were suspended without and within before the throne; all the courtiers put off their sandals outside the entrance into the hall, and stuck their long spears, which they carry about with them as walking sticks, into the ground close by them. Besides Mr. Richards and Aliheli, I took Friday our head Kruman and another into the king's palace, that they might see another court besides their own; as all the courtiers sat on the ground, we did the

same close before the king. He was richly dressed
in tobes made of broad yellow and green silk rib-
bands, and a rich yellow cashmere cloak, all of
European manufacture, thrown over the tobes, and
a rich carpet was spread at his feet. He had on
a native cap, wrapped round with a white turban,
and was seated on a mud bank richly adorned,
which served for a throne. He was about forty
years of age, thin in person, and rather darkish in
complexion, but of an intelligent countenance.
As soon as we were seated before him, he saluted
us many times over, in the Filani language, which
Ibrahim interpreted in Haussa, and Aliheli into
English.—He was very glad to see us. It was true
he expressed his wishes to see some one from the
white men's ship. His father had been king and
his brother succeeded him, but they never heard
of a white man's ship coming to their country,
nor had they seen any one from the white man's
country, as he had seen us. He thanked God for
this peculiar favour; and now he was ready to hear
what message we brought from the king of the ship.
—I then told him that our Queen had heard of his
kingdom a long time, and of the large river which
runs through it, as well of the Kowara which runs
through Yauri and Rabba; that ships have visited
the latter several times for the purpose of trade,
and that it was the Queen's wish also, to see
whether this river was as navigable as the Kowara,
and for that purpose had sent the Sariki of the
ship to see what sort of water it was, and the
countries through which it runs, as well to make

enquiry after a white man who had visited Yola
sometime ago, and returned to Sokoto, but promised
to return to some part of the bank of the Binue
to wait for the ship : that the king of the ship
hearing of his wish to visit the ship, had sent me
to invite him on board, and would be very glad
to see him.   I particularly urged him to get his
subjects to cut wood for us to buy, and said that
we would purchase about three hundred loads, in
hopes of getting at least half that quantity if possible.   There was plenty of dry wood in the way
to Hamaruwa, but at the distance of five or six
miles from the river, which made it difficult of
carriage.   He had not heard of Dr. Barth's visit
to Yola, but knew that a white man was at Sokoto
about two years ago : as to the river, there is he said,
always plenty of water till next moon, when it would
begin to fall and become very shallow.   He wanted
to know whether the ship intended to stop here
and trade, or to pass higher up, that he might
know what directions to give ; but if any thing
should happen to her, he should be blamed by
Sariki Mussulmins (the king of the Mussulmins,)
the Sultan of Sokoto, for neglecting to give proper
information.   I told him when he saw the Sariki
of the ship, they might enter into those particulars.
As to trade, he promised if the ship would stay,
to get as much ivory as she could carry in a short
time.   He excused himself from visiting the ship
at this time, saying, that as he has seen us, it
was as good as if he had seen the king of the
ship himself, and he was very thankful for my

coming at his request. I urged that it was worth his while to visit the ship, which indeed was like a large house, as Ibrahim could tell him from actual knowledge; but he declined, and said he would think of it by the time the ship returned from Adamawa, if she was going up, and that he would communicate with the king of the ship by writing, respecting the water and the country between this and Yola, which was hostile to the Filanis. I then called the king's attention to the Heathen population in his territory, who I perceived still continued in their idolatrous practices. I told him he was aware we were Anasaras, and they Mussulmins, and asked whether he would have any objection, if trade should be established between us and them, to our making an attempt to teach and civilize the Heathens in his territory, according to our way? With a smile he replied, that it was all the same, he was willing: the smile, in which his courtiers joined, seemed to imply,—you may try if you can succeed. I then presented him with the red cloak which Dr. Baikie gave me for him, and told him that I would report every thing he had said to the king of the ship. But he had been told by some one of the wonder I was performing in writing without ink, and yet, an impression was made on the paper; he therefore requested me to write that he might see: I stepped close to him, and wrote *Sariki Hamaruwa*, (the King of Hamaruwa,) and he was not a little amused to see the words drop on the paper as the pencil moved on. Having closed my interview with Mo-

hamma by this wonderful performance, I left the
court with heartfelt gratitude to God, for the success we had met with.   Ibrahim remained with
the king, and requested me to wait for him at
home.   I had told the king that I must return
to the ship immediately, because I had not had
an idea of the distance, and was expected on board
last night, and that if we did not return soon, the
anxiety of the gentlemen would be increased as
regards our safety.   We waited till noon, but no
letter from the king had yet arrived.   Ibrahim
returned, and told me to wait a little more ; and
about one P.M., thinking it would facilitate our progress, I sent the Krumen away with two men
from Ibrahim, to lead the goat and sheep onward
till we should overtake them.   I began to fear
we should not get on board to-day, even if we
succeeded in getting to Wuzu on the bank of the
creek : in short it was not till three o'clock that
the letter was got ready, and brought to my lodging, where it was read by the mallam who wrote it,
and interpreted to me by Ibrahim in Haussa.   The
king wished me to come to the Palace before
I left the town, which I did in my way; and I
waited outside, while he ordered Ibrahim to present me with a blue tobe of country manufacture, which was put on me, and a large blue
country cloth for Dr. Baikie.   They had been trying
to catch a bullock for us to take to the Doctor,
but the animals were so wild, that they could not
succeed, but he promised to send one in a day
or two.   He replaced the lost honey by another

pot; and a calabash full of fresh milk, and about
two pounds weight of fresh butter were added to our
presents; thus I took leave of Hamaruwa.   On
the way, I was told that the king was very glad
indeed to see us, otherwise, we should not have
had so early an interview; that many times, messengers from the interior had to wait thirty days
before they could see him; that after we had left
the palace, he sent one slave out to barter for
three tobes to present to us, but the maker of the
tobes was unwilling to give more than two tobes for
one slave; and that the king was obliged to borrow
the one he presented to me, hoping to be able to
get the other two for Mr. Richards and Aliheli,
when we returned again to Hamaruwa.   I was
glad at last to get on our way; but I doubted
very much whether we should be able to reach the
ship that night. It was not till eight o'clock P.M.,
that we reached Wuzu, and I was glad to meet
the Krumen all there in safety.   I told Ibrahim
to make ready for our embarkation for the ship,
but he was afraid of being attacked by hippopotami in the night in the bush, through which we
made our way to the creek yesterday morning.
As there was no alternative, we consented to pass
the night at Wuzu, though we had nothing to eat,
but a little dry Indian corn which the Krumen
parched for their supper.   Wuzu being infested
with musquitoes, not one of us had a wink of
sleep till day-light, every one being occupied all
night in brushing away the swarms of these insects
from their persons.   In and out of the house the

pest was the same; so that I sat with the Krumen
near the fire which was kept up by three sticks,
and constantly fed with grass till break of day.
Although we had no change of clothes, and no
covering, except what we had on when we left
the ship, with which we waded through the water
in our way to and from the town; we were better off
than the Krumen who had nothing to protect their
naked persons, and so they were more annoyed
than we were. Towards cock-crowing, the cry of
a wolf was heard a short distance from us. No
doubt it was attracted by the scent of the sheep
and goat tied in the yard where we lodged; the
men had told us that the creatures were not safe
where they were, but as we had no where else to
put them, I left them to the chance of escaping
during the night, or being carried away by prowling
wild beasts. I sat down close by, actually watching
whether the wolf would come after the sheep, not
to defend them, but merely to witness the attack
in the habitation of man;—the fire kept blazing
by the Krumen seems to have kept it off. When
going to Hamaruwa on Friday, the carcase of a
horse shot by mistake in the night by the farmers,
was lying close to the road, but on our return
next day, it was gone, carried away by the hungry
wolves; so numerous are they, that the people go
about always armed, ready to defend themselves
against their attack.

September 24 : *Sunday.* As soon as it was day-
light we hastened into the boat. The river has
risen very much since Friday, so that the creek

has become an expansive sheet of water, and we were enabled to make a short cut into the main river, and about half-past seven o'clock, A.M., reached the ship to the great joy of all on board. Many and various thoughts had arisen about us, and every additional day and night of delay increased the anxiety. The joy was more than could be expressed in words, when they saw us arrive in safety, and with a good report of our reception. As the king had refused to come on board, Dr. Baikie at once determined to set out on a visit to his majesty. Having given him every information that he might prepare himself for the journey with less disadvantages than we, he, accompanied by Dr. Hutchinson and Mr. Guthrie, the chief engineer, left the ship about noon for Hamaruwa. At two P.M., I kept the afternoon service, and read the first part of the second Homily upon the Fall and Misery of Man, &c.

The town of Hamaruwa is beautifully situated on a hill, rising on the south side of the range of the Muri mountains on the west side of the Binue. It commands a fine and extensive view. The river is seen stretching along like a narrow strip of white cloth, between the shades of light green grass, which fringes the water's edge, and a little further back is the darker green of trees, and then the blue ranges of Fumbina, with the lofty Mauranu mountain in Adamawa, on the left, and the Muri mountain in Hamaruwa, with their many fanciful peaks, on the right side, each at a distance of twelve miles from the river. In the valleys below the town, from one to two hundred beautiful cattle were feeding, and this gave life to the scenery. The houses are round, with conical roofs, built mostly of mud, about twenty or twenty-four feet in diameter. Many of these round houses are built in the premises of each master or head of a family, and enclosed with platted grass or fences which screen the whole group from the gaze of passers by. A narrow public street runs from one end of the town to the other, fenced in on both sides with grass, with now and then a lane or cross street. Except where the fences had been neglected, the inner yard of a group of huts was not visible from the street. Now and then the front of some premises is open to the street, and the people pass their time there in the heat of the day, under the shade of trees. If the town of Hamaruwa were regularly laid out, according to the plan of a civilized country, it would present a very delightful appearance; but at the time of our visit, many houses had fallen in, and the sites were overgrown with grass; others were planted with guinea corn, while a large portion were only partially fenced in and cultivated. The town, though situated on a hill, with a rocky substratum, is yet sandy, and thus dries immediately after the fall of the rain; and though situated at the foot of the Muri range, yet is not so near as to suffer any inconvenience from it. At night there was perfect silence in the town, no singing or drumming was heard, and the absence of light in the houses added to the dead stillness of the night. The inhabitants have no palm-oil, shea butter, nor nut oil for lights, and their sauce is made with cow butter. Cowries are not used, nor any other medium of circulation, but all is done by exchange, as in Zhibu. I had not time enough to inspect their market, but I think it must be very poor, and nothing like those held on the banks of the Kowara, and westward to the sea-coast. They procure water at the foot of the mountains, at a distance of nearly half-an-hour, and it is brought by the women in earthern pitchers, borne on the shoulder, because the mode of dressing their hair, plaited like a ridge, does not allow them to carry loads on their heads; many, however, who are not so circumstanced as to keep their hair always dressed in that manner, bear burdens on their head. Very few goats and sheep were seen in the town, and no fowls; perhaps, all these creatures are kept at their farms under the care of their slaves, but from the difficulty of purchasing any for the use of the ship, I think they can possess very few. The difficulty in getting horses to carry us from Hamaruwa to the river side, may, in like manner, be taken as a proof that they do not possess many, or else they did not wish to hire out their war horses for such a journey. Their slaves are chiefly employed in their plantations of Indian and guinea corn; but there is very little rice, although thousands of bushels of the latter might be cultivated to feed millions of people, the banks of the Binue being particularly adapted for the cultivation of this plant, after the fall of its mighty waters. The

Filani themselves being military men, do not make
agriculture their chief employment. They are very
dirty in their apparel. It would seem that from
the time tobes, shirts, trousers, and other garments
are put on new, they are never wetted, except it
be by rain, till they are worn to rags. With the
majority, the tobes and shirts constitute their apparel by day, and their covering by night, and
the trousers are often used as bags, in which corn
or other things are carried. The reader may ima-
gine what an amount of filth and vermin is thus
accumulated. The females are cleaner in their apparel, and bestow more pains in plaiting their hair,
and ornamenting it with flat pieces of brass, and
lead, and copper rings, which are fastened on them
in a fanciful manner. Large brass, lead, or iron
ear-rings are suspended in their ears, and larger
and ponderous rings of the same metals are worn
round their arms, wrists, and legs, according to the
means of the wearers; these metals, and some silver
come across from the desert to the Bornu and
Haussa countries, whence they are purchased from
Moorish merchants, and brought to this part of the
country, the traders receiving in return slaves and
ivory. Many of the rings are manufactured in
Kano and Katshina, in the Haussa country, and
there are some Kano brass-workers even at Hamaruwa, who are carrying on their trade with much
success; some specimens were bought from them.
Dr. Baikie bought a pair of brass leglets, weighing five pounds, for which the man asked 45,000
cowries, the price of a slave, but he took much less.

Traders from Kano and Katshina visit Hamaruwa
in large caravans, and sometimes pass onward with
other parties to Adamawa, where they purchase
slaves and ivory, the former carrying the latter,
and both are sold to the Moors in Kano or Bornu.
There is a Katshina man here, who is trading for
an Arab in slaves and ivory. He is the merchant
who brought the suit of silk dresses and carpets in
which the king appeared on Saturday, and which
he sold to his majesty for fifty slaves. These have
not all been paid, but when that has been done,
another suit, still in the possession of the merchant,
will be purchased. The slaves are used at the same
time as beasts of burden, loaded with ivory, and
marched to Katshina, Kano, or Bornu; in this way
tons of ivory are yearly carried away from the
banks of the Binue, and the country is depopulated
by the slave-dealing Filanis. Sometimes the ivory
and slaves find their way to the west of the
Kowara, and thence to the coast. Two routes to
Yola from Hamaruwa were given us by Ibrahim;
the one of fourteen stages, of nearly a day's journey
each, round the Fumbina mountains, circuitous but
safe, being occupied by, or under the influence
of the Filanis, and the other very short, of only
four day's journey along the left side of the Binue,
but so dangerous, that a part of the journey
must be performed in the night. The part of
the country where the natives are hostile to the
Filani traveller, is called Zena, and its inhabitants
are said to possess many horses. The other unsubdued native tribes who are so much dreaded,

are the Batshama, Bula, and Dampsa. We have
been many times warned to take care of ourselves
when we come in contact with them; for they
are sure, we are told, to attack us, none of them
being able to speak the Haussa or Filani languages,
so that we shall not be able to communicate with
them. On the back of Muri range, behind the
town of Hamaruwa, are tribes of Pagans, called
Wuruku and Zangale, who are said to be cannibals,
and go about naked, some of whom have been
conquered, and are now subject to the Filanis.
Ibrahim was very proud of giving us the names
of the principal states under Filani governors, who
communicate direct with the sultan of Sokoto.
They will be mentioned with the route to Yola
in a subsequent page.

September 25 : A great number of people visited
the ship to bargain for clothes, in which they are very
deficient : for their knives, spears, bows and arrows,
rings, swords, wood, salt, &c., they asked for cloth,
and very little for other things in comparison. When
they were thus engaged, it was very difficult to direct
their attention to other things, every one being desirous to get what he could. Some rich Haussa
traders brought swords, tobes, &c., from Katshina
and Kano to be sold on board; the swords are said
to be made by the Gadamawa, whom I could not
otherwise make out than as the Moors of Gadamis.
The red silky wool is said to be brought by the same
people in its dyed state, and sold in the Haussa
country. In the evening, Mr. Guthrie arrived alone,

having left Dr. Hutchinson at Wuzu waiting for Dr.
Baikie, who had not then arrived.

September 26: About noon, Drs. Baikie and
Hutchinson arrived. Dr. Baikie travelled yesterday
alone, without a guide, and no horse. He missed
his way, and was benighted in the bush, so that he
was obliged to climb a tree, and pass the night in it.
During the night, he heard the cry of leopards not far
from him. The situation was a very dangerous one
in a country so infested with beasts of prey; and
we were all very thankful that nothing worse had
happened, as God has thus far prospered us in our
journey.

September 27: As there was no prospect of
getting wood, and the season was advancing, it
was decided that the steamer should proceed no
further, but Dr. Baikie and Mr. May took boat for
three day's sail higher up the river, leaving the
mate in charge of the "Pleiad" till their return
on Saturday. The other boat was sent to Wuzu,
to kill two bullocks which the king had given to
Dr. Baikie, for they were too wild to be brought
to the ship in the little boat. Both boats being
away, we could not communicate with the village
till nearly the evening; when the mate went on
shore, and came back, with a report that the river
was falling. The apparent fall, however, was merely
the cessation of the rapid flow, occasioned by a
sudden copious supply from heavy rain, and, in fact,
the river had not yet arrived at its height.

September 28: Early this morning the mate
went on shore again, and reported that the rive

had fallen two feet, and that he had been informed that it would not rise higher this year. Those interested about the ship advised her dropping down at once. I did not like leaving the two Government officers behind, among a strange people in an unknown country. If anything should happen to them, how were we to know of it at Zhibu, a distance of upwards of one hundred miles down the river, where it was proposed we should wait for them, trading meanwhile with the natives? The result proved, that the "Pleiad" might have stopped a fortnight longer off Gurowa; but under the circumstances, it was thought better to weigh anchor, and the ship began to drop. While the steam was being got up, the boat was sent for all hands from shore, and thus I was disappointed of my purpose, to spend some time on shore to ascertain the religious rites of the people, and by quiet conversation to collect as much information from them as I could. On Tuesday night, a buffalo, a leopard, a crocodile, and some ground pigs killed by some hunters, were brought to the village of Gurowa. No sooner had the hunters arrived with their prey, than shoutings, loud cries, and shrieks were heard in the village, in praise of the gods who had thus given them success in their expedition, and a great part of the night was spent in singing and drumming. The heads of the animals were cut off, and dedicated to the gods as their portion, being placed in the front of the gods' house. All Wednesday was spent in the same manner, shrieking and crying the praises of the

gods. The head of the crocodile being a fine specimen, Mr. Dalton persuaded the hunters to sell it,
but he had to pay a good round sum before the
gods could be deprived of their rights. Although
the village comprised no more than thirty or forty
huts, yet it had two or three gods' houses. I asked
a Haussa man resident in the place, whethei
none of the Djuku, who are Filani slaves in thir
village, ever embrace Mohamedanism? He said,
No, never. I asked why they were not taught to
worship as the Filanis do? He replied, Are they not
slaves? There is some improvement among them,
however; and their females have substituted cloth
for the leaves observed at Tshomo and other places.

With little steam the "Pleiad" ran down the
river like a shot; in nine hours we made between
sixty and seventy miles from Gurowa. All the
high banks were completely covered, the river must
have risen seven or eight feet since we went up
about ten days ago. The country was flooded, on
an average two miles inland, to the foot of highland on both sides of the river; creeks and large
collections of lakes were visible to a great extent on
both sides, and this, in part, may account for the
absence of towns and villages immediately on the
river's banks in this part of the country.

September 29 : As there was no wood, we kedged
down the river, which was difficult, on account of
the number of islands, and the ship would not answer well to her helm without steam, though the
fan was unshipped. Unfortunately, about four P.M.,
she drifted abreast of an island, and stuck fast in

the mud, with a strong current on her starboard broadside ; attempts were made, but she could not be hove off this evening.

September 30 : Last night a terrific tornado blew, with copious rain, thunder, and lightning ; the ship was dashed against the bank with great violence by the strong wind and current, and driven more on to the bank. I felt less for our own situation than for those whom we left higher up in an open boat ; however, they were resigned to the care of that kind Providence by whom we have been preserved to the present time. Efforts were resumed to get the ship afloat ; every combustible material that could be spared, such as empty boxes, casks, useless paddles, &c., were split for fuel to get up steam to assist manual force, but, unfortunately it was discovered that the bilge injection was blocked up with the mud, so the engine would not work. The little steam was, therefore, blown off, and the only chance of getting afloat now, depended upon our personal exertions ; but nothing was effected to-day. From the rains of last night the river rose very perceptibly, and this gave a good hope of success, though some began to entertain doubts of it, and to talk of her probable abandonment. Three canoes were seen on the other side of the river, but they would not come near us.

October 1 : *Sunday.* The labour of getting the ship afloat, was resumed early this morning ; the Krumen worked hard, but repeated failures after many laborious attempts discouraged them much. The fear that she might have to be abandoned was still entertained by some. I felt still more uncomfortable on account of Dr. Baikie and Mr. May who were left behind, and was very anxious for their return in safety. At noon, when we were at lunch, the Krumen, who likewise had been anxiously looking out for the return of their countrymen with the boat, gave loud cheers when they saw it coming at a great distance. We were all instantly on deck, and were glad to see the whole party safely on board. They had made a voyage of thirty miles higher up the river from Gurowa; and reached the following villages :—Tshomo, a mile from Gurowa on the right side; Lau, higher up on the left, Bandawa, Djin, Abiti, and Dulti. The people call themselves Baibai, the same as the Djuku, or inhabitants of Kororofa. Batshama on the right, and Dampsi on the left, are independent of the Filanis, the other places are more or less under their control. They remain in their wild and uncivilized state; at Dulti they live like amphibious creatures in their flooded village. Their propensity to pilfer became manifest from their rude familiarity, handling every thing about the gentlemen more than was pleasant, and an attempt to stop the boat, was a sufficient warning for the explorers to get out of the midst of this people with all speed; while they were making their way out of the grassy creek, the natives pursued them in the canoes, if possible, to seize and detain the boat, with a view no doubt to plunder them ; nor did they return from pursuing them, till the boat had fairly got into the open river. Our party returned to Gurowa on Saturday morning, and were quite disappointed

at not finding the " Pleiad" there ; but they received
notes informing them of the cause, and apprising
them of our intention to drop down to Zhibu.   They
weathered the heavy tornado of Friday night in
the open river, exposed to the inclemency of the
weather, rain, thunder, and lightning.   On Saturday,
they attempted a new passage through a creek
which they supposed would lead them to the main
river a short distance below, but instead of this,
they were led to an extensive lake formed by an
immense spread of water over a large space of
ground on the left side of the river, and here they
were obliged to pass the night, not reaching the open
river till about half-past eight A.M. to-day.   After
not much more than three hours' pull, they saw the
" Pleiad" at a distance, which they suspected was
aground.   We had much cause for thankfulness to
God for bringing them back safely, after passing
four nights in an open boat.   All efforts to get
the ship afloat to-day were fruitless ; in consequence
of this, we could have no service.   At half-past
seven P.M., I read the Evening Prayers in the saloon,
but only some of the officers could attend.

CHAPTER IV.

October 2. The labour of getting the ship afloat, was resumed with the united efforts and assistance of Mr. May and Dr. Baikie; and to the joy of us all, our object was effected about three P.M.; the continued rising of the water greatly assisting us. At noon, a canoe was seen pulling up, and stopping among the grass to look at us; she was hailed alongside: she came from Zhibu, about twenty miles below us, and had on board as passengers, two Haussa traders, men of Bautshi, who were returning from Zhibu with two slaves and some ivory which they had purchased. The

ivory was bought from them in exchange for cowries
and some goods; the slaves sat in the canoe un-
shackled, as there was no chance of their escape
when travelling on the river, but they had on board
the irons to secure them, two pairs of which were
purchased by Dr. Baikie. The canoe had to pass
the night among the bushes, because there were no
villages near the water-side for them to put in.   I
asked about the population of this part of the
country, and was told that from Zhibu to the Akam,
or Kankundi river, and five day's journey inland
from Zhibu, no human habitation is to be found.
I asked, what had become of the inhabitants? They
replied, they had all been carried away captives
to Sokoto.   I asked of what nation were the slaves
they had on board; and they said they were Baibai,
of the town of Gomkoi, a tribe of the inhabitants
of Kororofa, who had retreated into the interior, and
there maintained their independence in some hilly
localities secure against the inroads of the Filanis.
They said travellers must sleep five days in the
bush before they reach Gomkoi.   I asked whether
the people of Gomkoi had horses; they replied,
that horses are taken across that way from Bautshi,
and exchanged, five slaves for one horse.   I showed
them pieces of iron, called " Kantai," which I got
from Hamaruwa, the use of which, I had not the
opportunity of learning at the time.   They said,
they were used as currency, one hundred such
pieces, being the average price of a slave.   I asked
whether the inhabitants of Gomkoi were Pagans or
Mohamedans: and was informed, that they were

all Pagans; that the males wore some sort of cloth around their loins, but the females, only a few green leaves. On asking whether they were cannibals; I was answered in the negative. I then inquired the name of the country on the right side of the river. They said, Bautshi, and told me that we were nearly opposite the village of Dali, the smoke from which was visible; from Dali one goes to Dampara, and then to Wazai, and on to Yakoba. I asked what language was spoken at Bautshi, and they said, the Haussa and Filani, but that Haussa is the prevailing language, though the country belongs to the Filanis, and that Mohamedanism is the prevailing religion.

On their departure, I requested them to use the poor slaves kindly, the only help I could render to the poor unfortunate sufferers. When the traders were on board, a canoe was perceived issuing from the bush with five or six men in it; on looking at it with the glass, the people were observed busy making some strange gesticulations towards the ship, as if they were performing some incantations, whether for her detention or departure, or invocation to her as a deity, we could not learn. The men were marked with white chalk in long streaks on their bodies, as worshippers of the gods are distinguished at the time of their devotion. They had been in sight about an hour, when the canoe from Zhibu came up to them, and I believe spoke to them. In a few moments they left the spot, and followed the track of the traders up the river, and both were soon lost sight of.

October 3 : Started at eight A.M., to drop down, and anchored off Zhibu at seven P.M.; at eight o'clock, a gun was fired to announce our arrival, the town being about a mile from the river. The high banks we left about three weeks ago were completely covered, and the flat ground overflowed a considerable distance; the corn-fields, where the people stood to sell their articles, and the chief rode about among them to keep them in order, and where our Krumen cut wood for fuel, were now navigable for boats and canoes to the very foot of the hill where the town of Zhibu stands.

October 4 : Early this morning we dropped a little lower down, for the convenience of wooding. Dr. Baikie, not feeling quite well, requested me to communicate with the chief, and to tell him of our intention to visit Wukari through him, and to ask him to supply us with horses and messengers to take us thither ; a velvet shirt was given me for him at the same time. Having ascertained the possibility of visiting Wukari from this place, especially as messengers from the king of Wukari were here, I returned on board to inform Dr. Baikie, and that the final arrangements for the journey required his presence.

October 5 : Went to the town on the subject of our journey to Wukari ; everything seemed fair and promising, but the difficulty was about getting horses ; owners were not willing to hire out their horses for the journey, under an excuse that there was so much water on the road, and that if their horses made the journey, they would die on their

return. It took us some time to reason the chief out
of this pretence; he then said, they had not more
than five horses in the town, which we positively
denied to be true: he then said, we should have
three horses to take us to Zu, half-way between
here and Wukari, where we must stop overnight,
while the messenger goes to Wukari to fetch horses
to meet us. Zu is a market-place, where people
from Zhibu and Wukari meet for trading and return,
but it is not inhabited. I asked him whether it was
kind in him to let strangers from a far country sleep
in the bush for want of a conveyance, when the
journey could be made in a day without such ex-
posure? He had been coveting another sword from
Dr. Baikie, under the false pretence, that the one
which was given him three weeks ago was broken,
and sent to the blacksmith for repair. We asked to
see the broken sword, but it was never shown; and
thinking this a favourable opportunity to satisfy his
covetousness, he asked for three swords if the horses
were to take us to Wukari. He was told of the
unreasonableness of his demands, and we asked, if he,
alone, were to receive four swords, what we were to
give to others? However, the Doctor was willing to
sacrifice another sword to his avarice, and to pay him
in addition 20,000 cowries, to which he agreed, and
the messengers were particularly requested to be ready
with the horses early next morning, so that nothing
might delay us. Having completed our arrangements, we returned to the ship, but with some doubt
whether we should get the horses. We have made
up our minds, however, in case of disappointment to

perform the journey on foot, if we could procure a guide.

October 6 : Early this morning we left the ship according to promise, and went to the king's house. We found him sitting in the outer entrance talking with one of his headmen, and with a furrowed countenance, indicating sourness of temper and feelings of dissatisfaction. We saluted him, but our salutation was coolly returned. We then told him we were ready to start for Wukari, according to the arrangements of yesterday. He wanted to know why we did not go first to the Galadima, his chief officer, and come with him? We began to apprehend difficulty; however, a messenger was sent to call the Galadima, who came without delay : the chief then asked why we did not pay first, before we had the horses? We asked him whether he thought we were liars, or that we had come from our country thus far to deceive? After many vain and groundless excuses, it was proposed that the sword and cowries should be sent for from the ship, and the cowries measured before him, to show we had no intention to deceive. Dr. Hutchinson returned to the ship and brought them ; but no sooner did the chief see the sword, than he said, the sword he wanted for himself, but cowries were of no use to him, and that he must have cloth in their stead. This was sufficient evidence that he was deceiving us ; and we would have performed the journey on foot with the messengers from Wukari, but they were under his control. They said they were not ready, having to prepare their food for the journey; we offered to feed them

from our own provision, but they still shuffled, till at
length, seeing plainly that the king was befooling us,
Dr. Baikie determined to show his independence,
and told him that when the vessel next returns to
the river, it will go to Hamaruwa, and report his
treatment of us to his master; reminding him that
we were not his boys to be treated in a manner
so unbecoming a king. We then took our cowries,
and sword, and luggage, and returned to the ship.
Before we got into the boat, a messenger was sent
to call us back, but as we had been so much deceived, we would not listen to him, but told him
that if the king had anything to say, he should send
properly to us on board. About an hour after, a
canoe was sent with a message from the Galadima,
to call us back, intimating that he had been blaming
the king since we had left, for his bad conduct
to us. The messenger was sent back with many
thanks to the Galadima for his kind interference,
and to tell him the object of our visit to this country, and assure him that our intention in visiting
Wukari, was more for their advantage than for our
own. In proof of this, I showed him a tumbler, a
carving-knife, some biscuit, bread, and salt meat,
and asked him whether they were not superior to
their calabashes, Indian corn, and the rough-
made knives we bought from them for mere curiosity? I told him, moreover, that by hindering
our visit to Wukari, the king only acted against the
interest of the country in general, and that when he
had once deceived us, we could not believe him any
longer. A short time after, the Galadima himself

came off with the king's messenger and his own, to
mediate in person between us and the king. He
said that the king had done very wrong, and had
been blamed for it by him, and that he would
guarantee for our visit to Wukari, whether we wished
to start to-day, or to-morrow morning. Considering
the effort this generous-hearted man was making on
our behalf, after showing him the great interest we
took in the country, and explaining to him that the
conduct of the king was calculated to turn it into
another channel (as he evidently saw and acknowledged), we promised to consider the matter till the
afternoon, and then we would let him know our
intention. He begged of us not to disappoint him,
and desired us when we went to the town, to go to
his house, that he might accompany us to the king
and reconcile us, and then make arrangements for
our journey to Wukari to-morrow morning. He then
left the ship, with the promise of a visit from us in
the afternoon. The people were quite displeased
with the king's conduct towards us, and were at the
same time afraid to come on board to trade, as we
had left the town this morning in displeasure; but
the Galadima was told that our matter with the
king need not prevent the people's coming to trade,
and that they had no cause to fear. According to
promise, after four o'clock, I started for the town.
Mr. Richards accompanied me, and we went to the
Galadima's house. He was absent from home, because a man was being installed this day as *Sariki
n doki*, i. e. the king of the horsemen, or head of
the cavalry. There was drumming and war dances,

with horns blowing, and soldiers parading the town with as much excitement as if they were going to storm a city. The Galadima was told that we were come, and the whole train followed him to his gate. The warriors armed with bows and arrows, and spears, moved towards us in parties of six or ten with speed, and then made a sudden stop, shaking their weapons towards us with an air of great self-importance. The women stood by the fence shrieking their cry in praise of the Sariki n doki, who was riding a fine young steed belonging to the Galadima. The horse was led by a man with a cord in his hand, to prevent accidents among the crowd, as well as to save the Sariki n doki the trouble of watching his carrier, as to-day was to him a day of pleasure and ease. I had expected to see the people in their holiday vest, to-day being also Friday, the Alitshima of the Mussulmans, in which they partially abstain from their ordinary pursuits. I was disappointed, however, for with but few exceptions, they were as dirty and ragged as at other times. The procession passed on, and we entered with the Galadima into his inner yard, and he seated us in his praying ground, a space of about twelve feet square enclosed by four sticks, to discuss the subject of our visit to Wukari. He gave me many thanks for coming according to promise, and said that he had blamed the king much for his unfair dealing, that he only retains the title of king, but that he, the Galadima, was the chief manager of public business, that we might make ready for the journey to-morrow morning, and that we should give the sword, which the king desired for payment, with three measures of cowries (30,000), or, if we liked, three red shirts instead of the cowries. Our stock of red shirts was nearly exhausted, I, therefore, agreed to pay cowries instead. I then asked how many horses we were to have; he said he was sure of his own, and one from the king, but the owner of the third had not yet been asked, and it was not certain whether he would let it or not, but that the king would ask him, and pay for the horse. I wanted to know the certainty of obtaining the third horse, and whether the king would take the cowries he had refused this morning, and I suggested that it would be better to go and decide the matter finally before his majesty. He was in the shed, performing his devotions when we got there; and while we were waiting in the hall by a faint fire of two or three sticks, which gave more smoke than light—a specimen of a Filani lamp—the Galadima performed his devotions also; it was then about sunset. About ten minutes after, the king returned, and he and the Galadima had a long talk in Filani. He then thanked me for coming and made many frivolous excuses, laying all the blame upon the messengers, who were not willing to go, because they were not first paid. I asked what payment he wanted now? He said he wanted the sword, but not cowries, and if the cloth we would pay him was good, he would take it. I asked how many horses we were to have? He said, he was sure of his own and the Galadima's, and that he would try to speak to the owner of the third this

evening; that we might hear the result when we
came in the morning. I told him we had spent
three days already in talking about going to Wukari,
and had been disappointed; if I were to go to the
ship, and tell the gentlemen to make ready for the
journey, and the horses could not be procured, or the
quality of the cloth for payment were to be disputed,
what were we to do? And meantime, the sun would
be as high as it was this morning, which was one of
the objections made by the messengers. However,
without further bargaining, I told him, I would
report what he had said to my Sariki, and he would
decide for himself. By the time we passed the gate
of the fortification, about seven P.M., it was being
fastened with sticks piled across the entrance; so
that we had to climb up and jump outside. At this
hour, none of the inhabitants were seen outside the
town. As we were walking towards the town with
the Galadima's messenger, he showed me the mark
to which the fortification was to be removed, about
200 feet in advance of the present: and said the
new sticks we saw at the water side were for it.
This made me inquisitive as to the need they had to
fortify their town? He exclaimed in Haussa, "*Ah
Wukari halbi;*" i. e., Ah, Wukari shoot arrows!
As I did not wish to lose a single word of what he
was going to tell me about Wukari, I called Aliheli
to me, that he might hear all perfectly. I asked
him to proceed, but he was on his guard; and said,
when the first attack was made upon this place from
Hamaruwa, the inhabitants of the towns, whom he
called Zuntu and Garba, resisted for ten days before

they were conquered, and since that time Zhibu had
had four kings—two had died, and the third was
too old to do business, and resigned the kingship to
Zumbade, the reigning sovereign.   In the mean
time we entered the town, and the subject was
dropped. The people of Gandiko had told us that
they had had war with Wukari, and were not able
to conquer it, but had remained there since. The
chief of that place made the state of enmity between
them an excuse for not letting us visit Wukari from
their town. The great distance between Zhibu and
Wukari keep them one from the other, though there
is a neutral market at Zu, where they meet at
times for trade and barter. Though they exchange
messengers one with another, yet the fact that the
space of a whole day's journey is without inhabitants, shows plainly that their professed friendship
is a hollow one. I returned to the ship and reported
the results of my visit to the Doctor; and the way
not being clear for our proceeding to Wukari, the
attempt to reach it from this place was given up.

October 7 : Mr. Richards was sent to thank the
Galadima, and to tell him, that having lost three
days' already, we could not visit Wukari from Zhibu
at this time, as the water was falling. The Galadima was very sorry, and went with him to the
king to report the message from Dr. Baikie. Mr.
Richards said, the king, as a cunning rogue would
do, attempted to charge us with duplicity; saying,
that we had charged him with a breach of faith
yesterday morning, but now we had acted the same
part. Why did we now refuse to go to Wukari,

when he was ready? Perhaps it was because 30,000 cowries were asked. Truly, he would have been glad to have got the sword, but the king of Wukari would now suspect him of hindering the white men from paying him a visit. In this and many other ways he tried to clear himself from blame.

October 8 : *Sunday.* Had service at ten A.M., and read the second part of the second " Homily on the Misery of Man, &c." All hands rested, and it was the most quiet Sabbath we have enjoyed since entering the Tshadda. After six days' hard labour, the body as well as mind need rest on the seventh. God saw the benefit of it to man, as well the honour he claims to himself in separating that day as his own.

October 9. Having got sufficient fuel to take us to another wooding-place on our way down, at ten A.M. we started from Zhibu. The inhabitants who were busy enlarging their town by removing the fortification, stood gazing at us till we glided out of sight. When the present fortification is finished, Zhibu will be about four miles in circumference. About one P.M., we anchored off Gandiko, when Ama, the chief, immediately sent to salute us, and sent some Guinea corn as a present to Dr. Baikie, and the ship's company. This we returned by a few yards of calico. The face of the country about Gandiko was entirely changed by the overflowing of the Binue to the very foot of the high ground upon which the town is built.

October 10. Having given the people oppor-

tunity to sell what they had, we got under weigh
about eight A.M., and made for Anyishi, off which
place we anchored about two P.M. Here we had
the misfortune of losing our best anchor and cable
in seven fathoms of water ; the whole chain having
slipped from its fastening. It was a serious loss,
as we had now but one anchor and a kedge left,
two kedges having been lost before. Agbo, the chief
of Anyishi, immediately sent to salute us with a present of two fowls and some eggs ; and we promised
to go on shore and pay him a visit, which we
fulfilled after dinner. Anyishi is a small village,
situated on a hill rising on the west side of Mount
Herbert, and separated from it by a valley. The
town is rudely fortified by low mud walls and a
ditch, all of which greatly need repairs. The huts,
about forty in number, are scattered about upon the
hill, and the spaces between them are planted
with corn and other vegetables, in a very irregular
manner. We met the chief outside the group of
his huts, sitting upon buffalo and leopard skins.
We at first attempted to communicate with him
through Haussa and Djuku interpreters; but the
Djuku interpreters not being expert enough,
the chief himself addressed us in the warmth of
his heart in the Haussa language. On Dr. Baikie's
mentioning that he was sent to enquire after the
welfare of the country, and to see if there is any
prospect of opening trade with them, the chief
gave thanks ten times over, for he could not
express himself enough in words to convey the
feelings of his heart. When he was told of our

various attempts to visit the king of Wukari, and our disappointment, he was very sorry, knowing how very glad the king would have been to see us. He said that his people were much oppressed by the Filanis, and the Berebere of Zaria, and Lafia, who came across two years ago, and drove them away from their old town, Sundube, from whence they took refuge at this place; that when they lived undisturbed in their homes, they hunted elephants; that at one time he had plenty of tusks, which he placed in a row in his hut like sticks, and spread his mat on them for his bed; that some of them were secured in his flight, others were carried away by the enemy, and the rest were burnt in the hut; and that they had lost many of their people, wives, and children. He pointed out one man from the five messengers, sent by the chief of Anufo, the neighbouring village, as a person who had been caught by the Filanis of Gandiko, whom they call Katshala, and who had lately effected his escape. He said that it was simply owing to such disturbance from those who were stronger than they, that they had become poor and have nothing. We asked the distance from Anyishi to Wukari, and he gave it as three good days' journey, namely, from Anyishi to Akwona about ten hours; from thence to Arufu or Afiayi, two neighbouring towns, twelve hours; from Arufu, or Afiayi, to Wukari, twelve hours. As the chief told us that he had sent to the chiefs of the neighbouring villages, who he hoped would come to see us to-morrow, we postponed leaving a message for the king of Wukari till then. Large lumps of leadore just landed from a canoe were seen in the town : it was dug at Arufu, one of the halting places to Wukari, where there is a mine, from whence it is conveyed to Keana, in Doma, for sale. Dr. Baikie purchased several large lumps, of from ten to eighteen pounds weight, for specimens.

October 11 : After breakfast we went on shore, to trade, as the canoes could not come alongside on account of the strong current—they had made several attempts, but were in danger of being upset. We took our seat under shady trees, when we were immediately surrounded by a large number of people. Trading was going on, on the one hand, while on the other, I was watching every opportunity of engaging the attention of some one in friendly conversation. Among the people around us, were some respectable-looking men, whom we recognised to be Mitshis, by the peculiar marks on their foreheads. One of them had a pipe which attracted my attention, and which I bargained for, and soon purchased with a razor. I asked where it was made, and was answered in the Mutshi country—for so they call themselves, while their neighbours called them Mitshi. I asked whether any Mitshi people were living in this place, when one of them introduced himself to me as the chief of a Mitshi village not far off, and several other Mitshi people were pointed out among the spectators. I engaged the attention of Njoro, the Mitshi chief, whose town is Iwom, not very far from Anyishi. Njoro spoke Haussa fluently, and as I had no interpreter, I tried to make myself understood as well as I could. When I told him that our Queen had sent this ship to see if the country was at peace, that she might think of open-ing trade with its people ; he interrupted me by asking, " What is the name of your king?" (for Queen) I told him ' Victoria,' which he made several attempts to pronounce after me, and said, " Your king is a true king; your king is a true king." When I told him that good people in our country always felt very sorry when they heard that people in this country fight and catch one another for slaves, which thing depopulates the country, and lays the land waste without inhabitants ; he burst out with enthusiastic rapture, shaking me by the hand, and asked for the name of our king again, as he had forgotten it, and said, your king is a true king ; and then with inexpressible emotion he addressed the Mitshi people who were there, in his own lan-guage, which of course I did not understand. He said they all belong to the king of Wukari, whom they were sorry we were not able to visit; that the king would have been very glad to see us, but that all they have heard would be reported throughout the country, which he said was very extensive in-land. I wanted to know the boundary between the Mitshi country, and that of Kororofa, but he said, by inserting his ten fingers between each other, that they were thus mixed together as one people—here is a Djuku town, there is a Mitshi village for many days' journey inland. I asked whether they all speak one language? when he answered in the negative. The Djuku language is quite different from that of the Mitshis I then requested him to give me the numerals up to twenty in Mitshi, which he did, and I pencilled them down in my note-book, to the astonishment of the bystanders. To cement our friendship, I produced a red cap from my bag, and placed it on Njoro's head, when all around shouted as a sign of approbation, for the honour done to the Mitshi chief. Here again I must acknowledge the kindness of Lady Buxton, by whom I was furnished with this useful article, as well as many others. Dr. Baikie returned on board, as Mr. May was coming on shore to take some observations, so he gave me a message and present for the chief of Anufo, the neighbouring village, whose messenger had just come to lead us thither. Dr. Hutchinson and myself then started for Anufo. The path lay between hills and valleys on the back of Mount Herbert, very close to which we passed, the soil is rocky and poor on the hills, but black and rich in the valleys, where Guinea corn flourished greatly. Just before we entered the town, we observed a small portion of land sown with beni, a very useful produce for commerce, which might be extensively cultivated here, as might cotton also, if the inhabitants were permitted to be at rest, and a market were opened for the produce of the country. The town of Anufo, situated on a small hill on the east side of Mount Herbert, about two miles from Any-ishi, is a neat village, clean and airy, fortified with walls and ditches around it. We were seated under a shady tree, waiting for Mr. May, who, we expected would come after us when he had finished his observations, and had been there about an hour, when

Abiki, the chief, sent for us. He was quite a young man, sitting on buffalo and leopard skins under a shady tree outside the group of his huts. After the usual salutation, we took our seat and commenced business. The chief's Galadima, or next headman, acted for him. The conversation was carried on in Haussa, interpreted into Djuku, although I believe he understood Haussa as well. In the meantime, Dr. Baikie sent me a note by Mr. Dalton, with a message to the king of Wukari, expressing his regret at not being able to visit the king this time, and a hope, if the ship came out again, that he might be able to fulfil his wish next year. This message I delivered, stating the objects of our intended visit under two distinct heads, for the easier digestion of his majesty : first, I said, we wished to know whether he was truly desirous that a treaty of legal trade should be made between him and England : and secondly, whether he would not like, at the same time, that his people should be taught to learn God's book, and worship God as we teach people of other countries ? To both of these questions, the Galadima, and a man from the king of Wukari, who was shortly to return thither, gave separate answers, as conveying the wishes and feelings of their king; but promised that the message would be faithfully delivered. They hoped God would keep them in safety till the ship returns next year, for they are always in doubt when they have passed one season without molestation, whether another will be as favourable, and said that in all probability we might not meet them

here next year. I encouraged them to look up to
God for protection, and told them, that many good
people in our country pray for their preservation,
and that war and the slave-trade may cease from
the face of the earth. I gave the presents from
Dr. Baikie, for which we received a kid in return.
Njoro, my Mitshi friend, had returned from the
ship, to which he was taken by Dr. Baikie, and
followed us to Anufo. We asked whether horses
could be got here, to make the journey to Wukari,
should the gentlemen return next year, and wish
to do so. Njoro replied, that ten horses could be
got, if we wanted as many. He was anxious that
we should visit his village, but it was too late,
being nearly four o'clock. Since we entered this
river, this is the first time we have come direct
among the oppressed inhabitants without being immediately under the watchful eye of their Filani
oppressors; hence they were free to lay their griefs
open before us, and to desire the friendship of the
white men, as the friends and well-wishers of all
mankind. Though Anju, the king of Wukari, pays
tribute to Bautshi, yet being a Djuku by birth,
he sought the protection of his people, and they
in return have an affection for him as their lawful
sovereign.

At Zhibu and Gandiko all the Djuku people,
though under the Filani as slaves, were very anxious for us to visit Wukari. They dared not say
it openly before their masters, but they were open
and free enough when they came on board. The
man from whom I collected a few Djuku words

to compare them with Koëlle's specimens, whose
name is Anju, the same as the king's, was ready
to accompany us to Wukari if we should deter-
mine to make the journey. Zumbade or Bohari,
the king of the Zhibu district, Ama the chief
of Gandiko, and Garike of Gankera, are all of
Djuku race, but have by usage become so amal-
gamated with the Filanis, by embracing their religion, and to secure their fidelity to the interest
of their masters, that they are placed in posts of
honour to govern the mixed population of Djuku,
and those who are half Filanis by birth, whom
they lead out to battle for their own interest, and
for the interest of their Sultan. They all go by
the name of Filani, but in reality they are not
so by birth, but by conquest and adoption of the
customs, language, and religion, of the conquerors.
We had not seen a real Filani, till we came to
the neighbourhood of Hamaruwa. This will be a
sufficient explanation of the hollow friendship between the inhabitants of the Zhibu district, and that
of Wukari; they are in fact the same people, but
the former have become instruments in the hands
of the Filanis to oppress their brethren, whose welfare and safety the king of the latter has at heart.
Should another expedition be sent out, and a visit
to Wukari be thought desirable, though the way
from Anyishi is long, yet if horses can be got, it
appears to me to be the best point from which to
make the journey, from among the subjects of the
king who take interest in the visit. An opportunity
would also be given of making accurate observation

in the lead mine in Arufu, and the country and people would be better known. Then again, as soon as the people of Gandiko and Zhibu see that another way has been found to Wukari independent of them, they will lay aside their vain and selfish excuses, and the nearest road-way— that from Gandiko is only about seven or eight hours' journey—will be laid open for future visits. Another inducement to the chiefs of these latter places, will be the advantage of the ship laying off their town for a much longer time, which they would lose by declining to promote such a visit to the interior.

October 12. Steam was got up as soon as possible, and for about an hour and a half, an attempt was made to fish up the anchor and cable, but in vain. It required steam to be kept up in full power to stem the current, which ran four and a half knots between Mount Herbert and Mount Adams, and we were obliged to give the anchor up for lost, and take our departure downward with the stream. In about four hours we made Rogan-koto, a distance which occupied us a day and a half in going up. We anchored off Rogan-koto according to promise, to give the people opportunity of trading, and also that we might get wood for fuel. We paid a visit to Jada, the chief, who was very glad to see us, and earnestly asked after our welfare. He said, that they were very much alarmed about us, because it was rumoured down the river that we had been attacked by the people higher up, and had had a dreadful battle. We told him on

the contrary, that we were welcomed in every place
we had reached, the great king of distant Hamaruwa not excepted, at which he was not a little
surprised. Here we met Onuse, Ojogo's sister;
she was the first to come on board, and give us an
affectionate salutation. She told us that Zuri, our
messenger, had returned from Keana, and was
at Ojogo ; the nature of the communication he
brought from the king of Keana she could not
tell, but no white man had come with him.

October 13. A great many people came on
board to trade in provisions, and various curious
articles, and plenty of wood, so necessary for the
navigation of the ship, was bought up. How
different the people of Rogan-koto from those of
Ojogo! The latter could not be moved to bring
a few pieces during the whole of the twelve days
we spent with them, whereas the former were all
readiness to supply us, men, women, and children,
turning out to bring wood; and all consequently reaped the price of their industry. In the
afternoon I walked to the neighbouring newly-
built village of Kondoko, which has been removed
hither since we went up, the people being driven
out of their old village by the rise of the river.
On my return from Kondoko, I fell in with two
Mitshi men at Rogan-koto, from whom I added a
few words to my collection, and gave each of them
a handkerchief. Among many other things brought
on board, was some rough beaten iron in the shape
of hoes. As I perceived they could not have been
intended for tillage, being entirely different from

hoes used for that purpose, and unfit for it, I was inquisitive to know their use. I was told that it is the currency of this part of the country, from Doma to Katshina, at which latter place it appears they are manufactured for trading purposes. Thirty-six of them is the average price of a slave, as one hundred Kantai are in Hamaruwa. This singular currency is called *Akika*, in Doma and Kororofa; *Ibia*, by the Mitshis; and *Agelema*, by the Haussas. I have purchased a few specimens which I shall send to England as curiosities.

October 14. Got under weigh at eight A.M., and anchored off Ojogo about nine, to take on board Zuri, who was our messenger to Keana, to enquire after Dr. Barth. The intelligence Zuri brought was, that the two white men, with their two servants, were said to have left Keana for Doma, and from Doma have gone to Toto, and thence to Abazhi, about forty-seven days previous to his arrival. How far this information may be correct, we cannot say; but we may have an opportunity of verifying it at the Confluence by enquiry from those who come down the river from Egga, or the neighbourhood of Rabba. We left Ojogo about twelve A.M., and anchored off Akpoko about three P.M., and landed to visit Magaji, the old chief, who received us with a hearty welcome, and was surprised to hear the distance we had made since we left him. The rumour that we had been attacked, and several of us killed on the upper parts of the river, had also reached Ojogo and Akpoko, and they were all thankful to see us return in safety.

October 15 : *Sunday*. Got under weigh at six
A.M., and anchored off Dagbo about eight o'clock,
where we stayed the remainder of the day, intend-
ing to wood here to-morrow. But the whole of
the farms, with all the houses, were under water ; and
the inhabitants had quitted the spot for their old
town on the back of the creek, that being now
secure against the Filanis, whom the water kept
at a distance. Had service at half-past ten, and
read the third Homily on the " Salvation of
Man," &c.

October 16. Some wood was collected from the
water, and cut ready for use. In the afternoon we
dropped down below Dagbo, opposite the villages
of Eruko, in the Bassa country, to which Dagbo
is subject. These villages had been visited and
burnt down by the Filanis a few months before, and
some of the inhabitants had escaped to the left
side of the river, while others fell into the hands
of their pursuers. The remnant have returned and
rebuilt their houses, and planted their lands ; but
one half of the buildings are falling into ruins,
because the owners are destroyed. As the king of
Bassa had returned from his flight to a small village
a short distance from the river, we purposed to
pay him a visit the next morning.

October 17 : Started early this morning in company with Dr. Hutchinson, Mr. May, and Mr.
Richards, after the rain, on a visit to the king
of Ikereku. There had been rain all night till
the morning, which made the road clean, and the
walk pleasant and agreeable. Two and a-half miles

brought us to the two small villages which at present go by the name of Ikereku, the capital, or residence of the king, the old Ikereku being about fifteen miles inland. It is said to have been more populous than Igbebe at the Confluence, and to be at a distance of four days' journey from Panda, and ten from Doma. Adama the king, is a middle-aged man, whose title is Agabi, the name of their old country Gabi, whence the Bassa people migrated to this part of the country; hence the title Agabi is taken by all Bassa kings. They were at one time the dread of their neighbours, to whom the Agatus, a tribe of Doma, were once tributary. Ikereku had been twice attacked before by the Filanis, but they were repulsed. But the Agatus, their dependents, were taken away from them at the conquest of Doma, by the Filanis. The late destruction of the Bassa and Panda countries, was brought upon them by Adama himself, according to their own statements. Usha, also called Afo and Ekpe, a part of the Bassas refused to pay tribute to Adama the king, and to punish them, he invited Ama Dogo, a war chief of the Filanis from Zaria, to attack them; an opportunity which was readily embraced by the latter. After the capture of the Ushas, according to the wishes of the king, Ama Dogo picked a quarrel with Senani the king's brother, who governed some portion of the Bassa country westward; and contrary to the king's wishes, they destroyed Akpatta, the town of Senani, and its dependencies; and as their avarice knew no bounds, Ikereku itself, the capital of Bassa, shared the same

fate; and thus the country was overrun, till Panda
was destroyed also. These particulars being related
by the Galadima, the next in influence to the king,
at the king's request, I could not help telling
Adama that it would have been better for him to
have lost the tribute of a few of his subjects
than to seek their punishment by the hand of their
common oppressors, and thus bring so much trouble upon himself, his people, and neighbours;—that
when a thief is employed to carry away a neighbour's goods, he will naturally seek opportunity to
carry away those of his employer also; and that
when an incendiary is engaged to set fire to a
neighbour's house, we are not sure that our own
will escape the conflagration. He felt the force of
these parabolical expressions, and said nothing; but
his subjects nodded assent to my remarks, and I
doubt not, he regretted the foolish steps he had
taken. The circumstance of the king of Bassa in-
viting the Filanis to destroy Usha, which was the
cause of the misfortune of Panda, explains the com-
plaint of the Igbira or Panda people, that the Bassas
had called the Filanis to destroy their country. Mr.
May delivered the present from Dr. Baikie to
the king, for which he gave a goat in return, and
pleaded poverty.

We returned to the ship about ten A.M., and
immediately steam was ordered to be got up. At
twelve A.M., we weighed for Abatsho; the place to
which a remnant from Panda had made their escape
about eight months ago, according to their own
reckoning. We arrived there in about two hours,

and landed to visit Mahamma the chief, who we heard was out of health. Besides the village on the water-side, there was another about a mile inland where the chief resided, to which a most pleasant walk through beautiful plantations of Guinea corn led us. The extent to which the plantations had grown in so short a time, told the industrious habits of the Igbira or Panda people. It is very much to be regretted, that such a people who are ready to turn everything to account, and who, if called upon to raise produce for foreign markets, would turn their whole attention to supply it, should be at the mercy of those who will not labour with their own hands, and are bent on enslaving those who do. Although the chief was not well, and rose from his mat with great pain, yet he did so to offer us his bed for a seat, and shook us heartily by the hand with inexpressible joy at our safe return—for news had reached this place also, that we had had a fearful battle with Filani warriors, and that there was great loss on both sides. He and his people were glad to hear that the reverse was the truth. He offered us eatables, and Guinea corn, beer to drink, and yams for a present. Since we have come among the Bassas and Igbiras, though they are oppressed, and driven to and fro by the Filanis, we may truly say we are among friends, and in the land of plenty. The country on the back of the river where Abatsho is situated, is dry; and the soil contains some clay with which some of the huts are built. Some parcels of cotton were purchased by Dr. Baikie and Dr. Hutchinson for specimens, from the industrious women who employ their time in picking out the seeds, and spinning the wool into thread, to be sold to native weavers.

October 18: Started early this morning, and about eight A.M., anchored off Amaran, on the left side of the river, near Mount Pleasant. This village was not visited on our ascent. It also is inhabited by refugees from Panda. A regular market is kept here every five days, and to-day being the market, we met a large concourse of people, both from the Confluence and upper parts of the Tshadda. The arrival of the 'Pleiad,' of course, interrupted their market, and in a short time the ship was full of people. Here we learnt, with no small joy, that Mr. Crawford and his party were well, in the canoe at the Confluence. Aba, the chief, immediately came on board, and he and Dr. Baikie exchanged presents. We landed, and purchased wood, of which they had plenty, and many curiosities, which no doubt gave a profitable return to their owners. The busy scene before us was indescribably amusing. After about two hours spent here, we weighed and visited the village of Oketta, on the right side a few miles below: here we met the sister of Oyigu, the late king of Panda, who was killed by the Filanis. The island on which the people of Oketta had taken refuge on our going up was completely overflowed, and the huts thrown down or washed away. Their old villages, on a long strip of bank between the river and a swamp, presented one complete scene of ruin and desola-

tion; yet within the ruins the weaver was quietly
pursuing his occupation, and the platter of mats
his work. As the Filanis still hang about the
country, it appears the ruins will be deserted altogether, and the inhabitants join their neighbours
at Amaran, near Mount Pleasant. The poor old
chief gave us some beer for a present. Starting
from Oketta, we dropped anchor for a short time
at Kende, where we made some stay at our ascent;
a short visit was paid them, and we then weighed
for Yimmaha, where we dropped anchor about three
P.M. The island on which the people had taken
refuge when we passed in August, was almost entirely covered, and they had returned to their town;
the high grass and swollen waters not being favor-
able to the expeditions of the Filanis; the inhabitants thus enjoying a temporary security from
these natural defences. The once deserted shore
of Yimmaha, where but four or five timid men
were watching the movements of the Filanis, was
to-day, lined by an immense crowd of men, women,
and children. The hearty welcome with which we
were received, could hardly be exceeded by that
of our most intimate friends in a civilized country.
We visited Ogara, the brother of the late unfortunate king of Panda, who is now elected in his
room, and is at present residing at Yimmaha. Rumour had also disturbed this place from Rogan-
koto, with news of our fabled battle with the
Filanis, at which they were not a little concerned.
The statement of Ogara, the king of Panda corroborated that of Adama, the king of Bassa, respect-

ing the invitation of the Filanis by Adama, to destroy Usha, which brought desolation upon them all. He said, the Filanis were now at war with Toto, that many of his people had only returned from that place yesterday, who went to ransom their children and relatives, and that some of the captives had effected their escape at the same time. As they had some ivory, the king requested us to return on board, that the people might sell it off.

October 19 : After breakfast we paid a visit to the king, and entered more circumstantially into the affair of the destruction of Panda, and the state of things between him and the Filanis at present. He confirmed the statement that Panda was destroyed by treachery, and said, that Oyigu, the king, had entertained them as strangers or traders who had come to his country, but when a sufficient force had got into the town, in the morning they commenced catching the people and plundering the houses. Three of the elders who had been caught, but have since been ransomed, and who were sitting by Ogara, were pointed out to us. Madaki, an elder war chief, who owned some horses, was dreadfully wounded in several places, in the act of defending them, and three large gashes now on his hand and back must have been severe. Oyigu, the chief, was killed, and the inhabitants taken prisoners before they were aware that any hostility was intended against them ; hence, all the dependent towns and villages were deserted, and the people fled for refuge to the island in the Tshadda, and to the other side of the river. Ama

Dogo, the Filani war chief, offered the condition
of paying one hundred slaves as an annual tribute ;
and the king said he feigned compliance with these
terms, till he had recovered as many of his people
from them as they were able to ransom ; and that he
would never go to Panda again, but when the dry
season comes will remove to the other side of the
river, and only inhabit Yimmaha in the rainy season, when it is difficult for the Filanis to get at
them. He said, if they complied and paid one
hundred slaves one year, in the next they would
require two hundred, and where were they to get
them ? and that they detested war, trade being
their chief employment. I asked him whether, in
case trade should be established with this country, he would like his people to be taught God's
book, and how to worship God as we do in the
white man's country; for it was these two things
together, which made England great, and that they
would bring peace and prosperity to any country
who received and embraced them. I told him that
the same thing was proposed to the chiefs of Aboh,
to the Atta of Igara, their sovereign, and to Mohamma, king of Hamaruwa, respecting the Baibai
or Djuku people, and that they were all willing to
trade, and that their people should be taught God's
book : I wanted, therefore, to know what he would
say to it also. He replied that trade was their chief
employment, and that he was very desirous that
war should cease, that his people might trade, and
be taught God's book : he wished us many blessings
and long life from the God whom we worship. He

said that he was a trader himself, and had been to
Hamaruwa, and that Mohamma, the present sultan,
was his friend; he had been to Zhibu, and knew
Bohari, the king, of whom he had a very low
opinion, but spoke very highly of the Galadima,
whose name he told us was Zumade, and that he
was a worthy character. We confirmed his testimony from personal knowledge and experience.
Dr. Baikie asked what portion of the captives was
now in the hands of the Filanis; he said, by far
the larger portion, and that as long as the army
kept together, and there was any prospect of the
captives being ransomed by their relatives, the Filanis would not sell them to others; but that would
not be the case when the army dispersed, and
carried their captives to their different homes. Dr.
Baikie enquired as to what might be the price
they paid for the ransom of each of their people ;
he replied, 80,000 cowries, whereupon the Doctor
offered the king that amount to assist him in the
ransom of one person, for which the king did not
know how to express gratitude enough in words.
He remembered Mr. Laird's visit to Panda, and asked
whether he was still alive, when he was told that the
same gentleman sent this ship to the river again.
Having taken leave of the king, and got under
weigh, about one P.M., we anchored, and visited the
village of Ogba, on the top of Frenchwood cliff,
which had been also deserted, but is now re-inha
bited. We landed, and climbed up the cliff. Kpanaki, the chief, was not at home, but we saw his
sister, a woman of some consequence, who is head

of the village. As her brother, Kpanaki, was living in the village Okpangana, on the opposite side of the river, a messenger was sent to inform him of our arrival, and he returned with the chief's brother, with a message, that he regretted that he was not able to come to the ship, because one of his wives died last night. Some presents were sent to him by Dr. Baikie, with words of sympathy: and after about an hour's stay, we started from this place for the Confluence, and reached the east point of Duck Island about half-past six P.M., when the water began to shoal to two and a-half fathoms. Fearing we might run a-ground, or upon rocks now under water at the juncture, we dropped anchor for the night.

CHAPTER V.

October 20 : Started early and anchored off the
town of Igbebe about seven A.M., in safety, where
we were welcomed by the crew of the canoe which
had left us nearly seven weeks ago. Their anchorage was very close to shore, and consequently,
exposed to the filth and stagnant water in some
pits, which rendered the place very unfavourable
to health. From this or other causes, Mr. Crawford was very unwell, and Mr. Gower, the second
engineer, in a very precarious state of health, but
all the natives were well. All the Europeans in

the 'Pleiad' enjoyed what may be called excellent health in Africa, and I may, perhaps, say more so than is enjoyed for a length of time together on the coast. Since we commenced the ascent of the Tshadda, no one who had any thing to do on shore had been idle, either in communicating with the native chiefs, trading, or in prosecuting scientific researches; journeys were made, for instance, to Hamaruwa, a distance of fourteen miles inland, by a very bad road, and without conveyance, exposed to every inconvenience, without suffering in the least from these exertions. Our Krumen and the native crew from Sierra Leone have suffered from sickness up the Tshadda, but the cause could not be assigned to the climate; it was from want of proper food, and over exertion. Their blood, consequently, from want of adequate nourishment degenerated, and they began to swell from their feet, with pain and weakness in the joints; but no sooner was their diet changed, than they regained strength. It is a hundred and one days to-day since we entered the river, and no death has taken place in the Expedition. Not unto us, but unto God, we give praise and glory. At noon we landed to visit Ama-Abokko, and to thank him for his kindness in giving us the messengers who accompanied us up the river; but from the tone of Ama, it appeared Zuri had told him how kind Dr. Baikie had been to the king of Panda, though he had rendered us no service, and yet the Doctor gave him so many cowries; while Ama, who did everything in his power to

aid us, was not half so well treated. Zuri had
also falsely asserted, that we had paid the messengers one measure of cowries only. We explained
the matter to the king, and promised to see him
to-morrow with Zuri, that we might expose his bad
conduct, which we would otherwise not have mentioned.

October 21 : On our arrival here on Friday, I
made enquiry after Dasaba, who was driven out
of Lade, and about the state of the country in
general. I was then privately informed that the
Yoruba of Ibadan, in our station near Abbeokuta,
were bringing Dasaba back to Lade ; that the town
was being put in order before Dasaba's entrance;
that Ama-Abokko and Dasaba were friends; and that
Dasaba had intimated to Ama-Abokko his wishes
to come down the river, and establish a town on
the land purchased by Government from the Atta
in 1841, a portion of which was let for the Model
Farm, from which place he would assist Ama-
Abokko against his enemies. I told Dr. Baikie
what I had heard, and suggested the expediency
of reminding the king that the place is Government property, and that he is bound to take
care of it for them, without alluding to what we
had heard. There was another matter connected
with Zuri, the messenger, for which we wanted
an interview with the king. On our arrival at
Ojogo, the ship anchored for a time to take him
and Mahamma his companion on board, but it required no little patience and forbearance, as well
as threats, to get him off : either some one was in

his debt, or he owed something which he wanted
to settle before he went on board. We threatened
to leave him behind, and take Mahamma alone to
the Confluence, in which case he would have to
account for himself to Ama-Abokko, whenever he
chose to return to him. In the hurry and confusion of getting them on board, as the ship had
got under weigh, he brought his two sons, Musa
and Bawalla, with him, and another little boy besides. He wanted four women, who he said had
come from the king of Keana, to come on board
and sell their rice, but we would not allow it, so
the canoe was let go, and they returned to Ojogo.
We knew Musa and little Bawalla to be his children, but the other little boy was quite a stranger
to us, so we asked who he was, when he replied
that he was a home-born slave belonging to Bawalla's
mother, and as she had left him to live with another husband, he took his son Bawalla away, and
this little boy was his companion. Had it been
otherwise, Dr. Baikie would immediately have ransomed the slave boy; and as the three little boys
were so happy together, we believed the matter to
be as it was related to us, but I continued to
watch if I could discover any cheat in the case. A
few days after this, Aliheli pressed Zuri to speak
the truth as to whether the boy was really a
slave intended to be sold away. The truth was
thus elicited that he was purchased by Zuri for
sale. Mahamma came to tell me the matter, and
said, as we had wished to ransom the boy, Zuri
would let us have him. As they did this igno-

rantly, I told Dr. Baikie of the fact, and the bargain was struck for the boy's ransom for 50,000 cowries. Among many other things, Zuri told Ama-Abokko that he had purchased the little boy for him, and that Mahamma had taken the boy from him, and sold him to us. Early this morning Zuri came on board to entice him away, but he was turned out of the ship, and told that he was fortunate not to be put in irons. After breakfast we went on shore, to have an interview with Ama-Abokko on these various subjects. I need not enter at length into the whole story; suffice it to say, that Zuri's misconduct was related to the king, and Ama was given to understand that we bore with him for the king's sake, and hence alone he had not been dealt with as he deserved. The barefaced lie, that he and Mahamma had been paid only one measure of cowries each, was alleged as an instance of his ill-behaviour; and he was forced to confess before the king, that we had paid two measures to each of them. Zuri thought, by reporting the payment of one measure, he would keep the other entirely to himself, while the king would divide the reported one with him. I then told the king, that when a man was guilty of such duplicity to his own chief, he might believe that he would tell other falsehoods. I asked Zuri if he had ever mentioned to us that he had purchased the little boy for the king, and he confessed he had not. Dr. Baikie said he would keep his word, and ransom the boy; but instead of paying Zuri, he would pay the amount to the king himself. He was therefore liberated for 50,000 cowries, and is now very happy with us on board. Zuri had been very serviceable to us, but his character was sadly stained by his addiction to lying and covetousness. I took the Blue Book containing the papers of the Niger Expedition of 1841 with me when we went to the king. Ama was reminded of the visit of the four ships, and of the purchase of the land for the Model Farm, together with the cause of its abandonment. He was then informed that Government had not forgotten the place; that we had been to see it, and found it all right, and we requested, as he was close by, that he would keep an eye to it, and see that nobody touch the land, giving him to understand, that we should report at our return the condition in which we found it. Ama-Abokko replied, that he was now the owner of that place, and that it must be bought from him. I replied, that it was not customary to pay twice for one tobe (holding at the same time the tobe of Daganna his Galadima), upon which he smiled. Dr. Baikie told him that he would go over the ground, and put up a flag there before we returned to the sea, to indicate that the land is still a British possession. I pointed out to Dr. Baikie the necessity of taking such steps to keep Dasaba from occupying it, for once established there, he would do immense mischief to the poor defenceless refugees on the left side of the Niger, at the fall of the river. Moreover, if portions of land were once built upon, and the best localities spoiled by their irregular towns

and villages, it would not be easy to clear it
when the place should be wanted for better purposes. I regret that the Model Farm was broken
up, though it could not have been otherwise under
the circumstances on account of which it was abandoned. The natives are still looking forward to its
re-establishment, more particularly for the purpose
of traffic.

October 22: *Sunday.* Held service at half-
past ten A. M., and preached from 1 Sam. vii.
9—12. Truly we have much cause for raising our
Ebenezer to God. All hands rested from labour,
and no trade was allowed to be carried on with
the ship, so the day wore the aspect of a Sabbath.

October 23, 24: The ship was full of people
trading with all kinds of articles: ivory, country
cloths, tobes, mats, shea butter, palm oil, yams,
sheep, goats, fowls, &c. Anything in demand,
either for curiosity or for use, was readily brought
for sale, for cowries, or in exchange for European
articles. The scene showed the disposition of the
people to trade, and that a trading establishment
at the Confluence would prove beneficial to the
country in general. The languages spoken here
are Igara, Igbira, Nupe, Kakanda, Haussa, and Yoruba. The Yorubas find their way to the Confluence by way of Lade or Rabba, from Ilorin. People
speaking Doma and Djuku, the language of Kororofa, also visit the market at Igbebe at the Confluence, and the Ibo traders come up as far as this
from the Delta. Among the things purchased as
curiosities, was a kind of fancy cloth, said to be

manufactured by the people of Igbo, south of Idda, near the Ibo country, who they said were like the Opú or Ibo, and their language nearly similar. Hence my attention was drawn to find out who the Igbos were.

October 25 : To-day being fixed for our departure from Igbebe, we went on shore to take leave of Ama-Abokko, and thank him for his kindness to us during our stay with him. The site of the Model Farm was particularly put under his care by Dr. Baikie, till steps be taken in due time to do something. I asked Ama-Abokko whether he would afford protection to any Nupe, Igbira, Kakanda, or Bassa people, who might be disposed to come over with the next Expedition, with the intention of settling in the country? He said there was plenty of room at Igbebe, and he would be glad to receive as many as were disposed to come; the only thing which caused him uneasiness was the unfriendliness between him and the Kakandas on the back of the town. We told him that we hoped when another ship came, and trade is opened, that those Kakandas would be spoken to, and that they would be friendly again. Ama-Abokko is quite willing that his people should be taught to read and pray to God, as we teach people of other countries. We shook hands with him, and parted with good feelings. Daganna, Ama-Abokko's Galadima, a Nupe by birth, is a worthy character. He professes Mohamedanism; and all the time the canoe was off the town, he paid every attention to it and its crew, that nothing might go wrong during our ab-

sence up the Tshadda. Since our arrival, not a
day passed when we went on shore, that he did
not invite us to his house, and entertain us with
Guinea-corn beer, which he many times poured out
of the pitcher for us with his own hands, though he
would not drink it, being prohibited by his religion,
nor, except for us, would he have touched it. This
and other things, as kola nuts, he would set before us, or anything else he thought acceptable.
He sent on board daily bowls of pounded yams,
and a pot of good sauce, which was very much
enjoyed by the ship's company. He was a busi-
ness-like man, and very orderly in his manners,
and obliging in his disposition. He was the last
on board, and when sent on shore in the ship's
boat, as we were getting under weigh, this young
and affectionate man was seen shedding tears at
parting with us, as if we had been old and intimate friends. All the people stood on shore, and
followed the Pleiad with their eyes till she was
out of sight. One of the sailors was the bearer
of a symbolical letter to a Nupe relative in Sierra
Leone. This letter consisted of a red parrot tail
tied to a white cotton thread at one end, with
a small piece of hard wood, burnt black at one ex-
tremity fastened to the other end of the thread, four
cowries being attached to the middle of the thread,
two facing each other, with the small ends upward, and the other two in like manner with the
small ends downwards. This may be interpreted
as follows : — the piece of hard wood burnt at
one end may mean, we are well and strong, but

have been mourning for your loss, and our hearts are as black as coal fire. The parrot tail may mean, we are all in good circumstances, and are expecting your return as soon as possible with the speed of a parrot. The pair of cowries with the small ends upward, facing each other, may mean, we wish to see you face to face. The inverted cowries may allude to the disorderly state of the country, as if all things have been upside down. These facts prove the willingness of the people for the return of their people, and their desire to enter into trade with the English; and with them before us, I hope some steps will be taken to aid the return of the natives of the Niger to their countries, as a beginning of future operations to improve the people. We anchored off the town of Agbedanma, situated on a hill, with Oko Odogbo below it on the left, and Otuturu on the right, on an island. Okeyin had removed his camp from English island to this place, on Abokko's people quitting the town of Idda, since we went up.

October 26: Dr. Hutchinson landed early this morning at Agbedanma, where he met our old friend Ehemodina from Idda, and brought him on board; he said he had come there thirteen days ago on a visit to Okeyin, who was his relative, and he could not forget him though involved in a dispute with a party, whom it appeared the Atta favoured. He was invited to breakfast, but he would not eat before his people, or at least till he had performed some religious ceremony which he called washing; but although he was taken to the

saloon where he might be by himself, yet he would
not touch anything. However, to oblige Dr. Baikie,
after he had touched the wine in the glass with
his finger, and rubbed it on his head and hands,
he drank that:—the meat and bread intended for
his breakfast he requested to be allowed to take
home, and it was accordingly wrapped up for him
in brown paper. His religious observances gave
opportunity for conversation on the religion of
white men, in which he engaged with much interest. Okeyin and his companions, who had also
come on board, took breakfast in the saloon which
they very much enjoyed. Okeyin being a brother
of Ama-Abokko, I related to him all that had
been proposed about the return of the Igara, Igbira, Nupe, and Kakanda people, from Sierra
Leone to this country, and he also promised, that
if they came, they should meet with a hearty welcome and full protection. Dr. Baikie then made
them several presents, for which they were thankful. Abokko's people are a powerful party, as I
have observed already under date of August 1.*
They are becoming independent of the Atta, and
I believe in a short time, if the present dispute
between them and Agabidoko is not soon settled,
they will shake off his yoke. They command the
market from Aboh to the Confluence. Aje of
Aboh seems to be in favour of Okeyin, and as
they are commercial in their disposition, Aboh
would go to trade with Abokko's people as far as
the Confluence, were they to remove so far up

* *Vide*, page 27.

the river. In consequence of this, the old Ikiri market, (the Bocqua of the Lander's) is at present suspended, or rather removed partly to Igbebe, where Ama-Abokko is now, and partly to Otuturu where Okeyin is encamped. Aboh traders attend both markets, the latter especially, while the people from the upper parts of the river, stop either at Igbebe or Otuturu as they please; but Agabidoko's party dare not go up to either of them, nor disturb Aboh traders when passing Idda for Otuturu. It appeared from all accounts, that these two contending parties are engaged in preparations for a conflict next month when the river falls. Time was allowed for the people to trade with us, and about noon we weighed for Idda, where we anchored in the afternoon, two guns being fired to announce our arrival. After five, we landed and walked along the edge of the cliff, but there is very little to interest a stranger. Many of the inhabitants having left the town, the houses were for the most part, empty; and long grass was growing between groups of huts which at one time were thickly populated. It threatened a tornado and rain, but we managed to have a few minutes conversation with the brother of a chief before we hastened back to the ship, just as it was getting dark.

October 27: Early this morning two messengers were sent to the Atta to announce our arrival, and to say that the whole day would be given to trade. No one felt any inclination to pay his majesty a second visit, on account of the difficulty and waste of time, which made the task unpleasant. The day was employed to better advantage on board, where people from different parts came together, and plenty of information could be collected. Our messengers did not make their appearance till late in the afternoon, when the Atta saw them, and promised the bullock offered on our ascent; but it was to be shot that evening lest he should get away by the morning. This made us doubt the sincerity of the Atta, because the bullock could easily have been secured till the morning. Since Abokko's people left Idda, there has been little or no trade in this place. The Atta however, wanted the ship to stop five days, to which we could not consent. The coals left near the water side by his permission and under his care three months ago, were found safe, just as they had been packed up by the engineer.

October 28 : A man was early sent to the Atta on private business, and the bullock, still alive, was delivered to him to be taken on board, but without any assistance being given him. The animal made towards the man, and he at once let him go to escape being gored; and thus the Atta's present was lost—a loss which did not concern us much, as it was not given with a willing heart. We landed early, as steam was being got up, on a visit to a chief who was on board yesterday, and had a long conversation with him on different subjects. As far as he could recollect, he enumerated twenty Attas who reigned in Igara, and said that the present, who is the twentieth, is now in the twentieth year of his reign. He gave a brief

account of the origin of the Atta, which is as
follows:—The part of the country now known as
Igara, was formerly Akpoto country, our informant being himself on the mother's side related
to the Akpoto. The name of the original king
was Igara; the first Atta came from the opposite
shore from the interior, and belonged to a tribe
named Ado, but called Idu by the people of Aboh.
His calling was that of a hunter, and whenever
he killed an elephant, or any other beast, he never
took any part for his own use, but delivered the
whole to Igara the king. Igara at first suspected
the proceedings of the Atta, but as he did no
mischief, and had very little power, not much
notice was taken of him. In the mean time, more
people came over from Ado and joined the Atta;
and when he found himself sufficiently powerful,
he refused to give Igara any more game. There-
upon Igara demanded the reason of this; and the
Atta gave an impertinent answer, that he had
given him enough already. A quarrel forthwith
arose, and the Atta drove Igara into the interior,
and became king of the Igara country. The
Akpotos we were informed, are now subject to the
Atta, and their language is the same. The chief
said, moreover, that the kings of Nupe and Aboh
also sprung from Ado, as did the Atta of Igara.
He also gave us information respecting the natives
towards the Ibo country, especially the Igbo, whom
he identified with the Opu or Ibo, which shall be
mentioned if the account be corroborated as we
go down the river. He was very glad to hear me

mention the intention of God's people to send their countrymen back from Sierra Leone to settle among them, and establish trade, and to teach them the worship of the true God as they have been taught in the white man's country. I spoke with him for a considerable time about God, and the folly of idolatry; and all I said was listened to by him, and all present, with much attention. We returned on board, and about half-past eight A.M. left Idda, and anchored off Ada-mugu in the afternoon, where we landed. This was a town of some consequence at one time, where Abokko lived, and where Mr. Laird buried thirteen of the crew of the Quorra, and two of the Alburka. It has declined since the death of Abokko, and nothing but the association of its name with that man, and with Laird and Oldfield's expedition gives it any interest. On our approach, the few inhabitants armed themselves with muskets, ready for self-defence, and looked upon our landing with great suspicion; but there was a Haussa slave there with whom we spoke, and he quieted their fears. Dr. Hutchinson asked for the graves of the white men buried there some years ago, but it appeared no one there had any recollection of the circumstance. There was one man who said he remembered the visit of the white men, but he was a little boy at that time, so he could give us no account of it. Their chief they said had been dead sometime, and his son had committed murder and ran away. Two among them were pointed out to us as their present chiefs, to whom Dr.

Baikie gave some presents. The first town was
flooded, and the stench of decayed vegetables was
sensibly perceived. We wanted to get to their
other town, but they told us we should have to
wade before we reached it, so we gave up our
intention. Dry-fire wood was asked for and readily
brought; and thus a little trade was carried on
with them. Some people had just come in their
canoes from some markets on the opposite shore,
with mats, said to be made by the people of Ado.
This mat is of the same pattern used by the Yoruba, and the Ijebu near Benin, from which I think
the district of Ado can be at no great distance.
They gave us some account of the Igbo people,
who they said were near the Opu or Ibo country,
and very much like them.

October 29: *Sunday.* Held divine service at
half-past ten, and preached from Heb. ii. 1—3.
Some canoes came alongside to trade, but they were
sent away, and told that no business is done on
this day, which is our Sabbath. There was a market
to-day, in a place called Utò, about a mile below
Adamugu, on the right side of the river. This
market is said to be attended by the people of Ado,
about a day's journey from the interior; and Ara
market, which is held at another time a few miles
below, is attended by the same people. Both Utò
and Ara markets were established by Abokko, when
he resided at Adamugu, but he gave Ara market to
Agabidoko to reap the advantage of it for himself;
hence Ara market belonged to old Agabidoko, whose
party is now residing partly at Idda, and partly in

the neighbourhood of Adamugu, and is at enmity with Abokko's people.

October 30: As soon as steam was up, we weighed from Adamugu, and anchored off Asaba, on the right side, where we landed; the people as at other places, were frightened at first, and held themselves in readiness for self-defence, but a few words of friendship and peace soon subdued their fears. The town of Asaba is situated on a gradual elevation, and the road to the top from the water-side is kept in good order. Immediately before entering the town, a spacious road, which could not have been less than thirty feet wide, led into the place, and from this road others branched right and left under shady trees to private dwellings, in groups of family houses. The town is by no means regularly laid out, but this is more to its advantage, as the houses are at great distances one from the other, which makes it airy. The soil is a red mould, with which they build their mud walls, and the streets are covered with sand and loose earth. We were led to the house of Ezobogo, their head chief, for there are many. The reception we met with here was beyond expectation, especially as they bore a very bad name among their Aboh neighbours, for they are Ibos. Without entering into particulars of their willingness to trade, and to allow their people to be taught the religion of the true God, of which I spoke with them for a long time—the dryness, and probable salubriousness of this place, which opens to the Niger, and is the best port to the Ado country, which seems to border

on Benin and Ijebu, make it the best calculated
for a settlement of any I have yet seen between
Aboh and Idda. The fine hilly country on the
back of Asaba, is called Oria, and belongs to Ado.
There are two small towns between the hill and
the river, whose market-places are Utò and Ara.
The natives speak Ado, Ibo, and Igara. Some
people from Ossamare reside at Oria, and are known
there by the name of Akpram. There are some
villages called Ugboru and Akpram, or Akpram
Ugboru on the right side, belonging to Asaba; they
paid tribute to the Atta formerly, but are now
independent of him. Inam and Onitsha on the
left side, and Asaba, used to be troublesome to Aboh
traders on the way to Igara, but could not prevent
their going, because Inam is the only place which
possesses canoes large enough to make effectual
opposition. There is also a small Ibo tribe on the
left side, called Isugbe, before tributary to Obi, but
now independent. A town called Asabutshi on the
right, above Asaba, was first inhabited by a man
who had murdered a man and woman, and fled
thither for refuge. None of these places are visible
from the river, but were pointed out to us near
Walker Island, or the group of islands thereabouts.
Their respective localities may be more accurately
determined hereafter. Among other places mentioned
is the Igbuso district, at the back of Asaba, having
two towns, Ogbori and Ogbobi. Uzugbe, Onitshi,
and Utu on the left, belong to Idda. These are the
names of different places between Adamugu and
Onitsha, given to us by our interpreter.

We weighed from Asaba, and anchored off
Onitsha market, where we had seen about five
hundred people in the market, on our ascent. To-
day was market-day, but we came too late, as it
was just broken up. However, we met a few
people, among whom was Odiri, the son of the
king, or Obi Akazua, of Onitsha town, which was
some miles from the market-place on the left side.
Here we made enquiry for the Igbo tribe, who
make the fancy country cloths, upon which Odiri
at once pointed to himself, and said, "We are the
people who make it." He told us, that the people
of Idda, and higher up the river, not knowing the
difference, call them all Igbo, which is the name of
a small town named Igbo Inam ; that their country
is called Igbo, but in fact, they are all Elugu of
Igbo, or Ibo, and that this is the market attended
by the Elugu people from the interior. He then
gave me the following names of towns in Elugu,
which attend Onitsha market, held every five days :
—Obotshi, Umu, Oja, Nkpò, Obba, Abadja Ezon-
ganran, where the fancy cloths are made, Abadja
Obba, Akuku, Ukè, Oto, Nnewu, Ozhi-Owere,
Obu, Ofu Abadja, Nkuere Nzhibe, Nteja. The
names of the different fancy cloths are Owowo,
Anaba Obiri, because made in Obiri, and Nwega.
I asked Odiri, how they would like to see their
countrymen now in white man's country, come
back and reside among them, and teach them what
they have learned during their sojourn in that
country ? He said, that as long as the white men
have it in their mind to introduce trade, whom-

soever they propose to send, would be welcomed,
and no injury would be done to any of their countrymen who might come to dwell among them. He
asserted that they never sold one another, but such
slaves only as are brought to them from the upper
part of the country. He was very anxious that we
should see his father; but we could not, as the town
was some distance off, and we were desirous of
getting to Akra-Atani that evening. Here we were
told, that the tribe of Isuama make Ossamare their
market-place on the river side. We left Onitsha
market with the intention of anchoring off Akra-
Atani, where we missed Aje on our way up; but
through the negligence of the interpreter, we passed
the place before we were aware of it; we, therefore made for Ossamare, but could not reach it
that evening, so we anchored off a place called
Osutshi, not visible from the river. I should have
mentioned that the country at the back of Onitsha
is dry, with rising ground, and this is said to be
the character of the country far into the interior,
with no water on the way. Asaba and Onitsha on
the opposite shores present the two most promising
localities to be inspected by those whose lot it may
be to commence missionary operations among the
Ibos. In questioning Aliheli, our interpreter, as to
the dryness of the country in the interior, and
whether the Elugu and Isuama have canoes; he
answered, "They cannot swim:" meaning, they are
not watermen, like the people of Ossamare, some
of whose canoes are so small, that they sit across
them, and stretch both their feet in the water, with

which they propel the canoe, as if a duck were swimming in a pond.

October 31 : Weighing early from Osutshi, we anchored off Ossamare, only a short distance from it, and went on shore. I was quite disappointed in this place, for it was a complete swamp. Although the river had fallen four feet, and the town was partly drained, the spaces between the houses, and the squares within them were all mud, and the heavy rain of last night made it worse. Between the houses immediately facing the river, and the king's house, was a puddle or swamp, with about four feet of water, over which were thrown some pieces of broken canoes, and some sticks tied together in the shape of a bridge to cross to the king's house. His square was more like a pigsty than the habitation of man; but the verandahs and rooms being raised above the level of the water were dry. We managed to get into the house of Nzedegu the king. After Dr. Baikie had told him the object of his visit to the river, I was introduced to him as one having something different to propose. I told Nzedegu the wishes and intention of good people in our country, to send their liberated Ibo countrymen back to their country, to teach them what they had been taught in the white man's country, especially the knowledge of the true God whom we worship ; that this proposal had been made to the chiefs of Aboh, the Atta of Igara, and other kings in the upper part of the country ; and that they all agreed to receive their returning countrymen, and to permit their people to be taught by them the worship of the true God. He replied, that whatever the chiefs of Aboh, and the Atta of Igara, had consented to do, he would do also ; besides this, that white men were their masters, and whatsoever they propose to them must be done. He said, the Isuama people attend Ossamare market, and that the country extends in the interior for many day's journey. After leaving the chief's house, I walked over the town, and looked into many of the houses, and found them all of the same character. When the water is high, canoes must be used in moving from one part of the town to another. Having seen the place, and heard the wishes of the chief, we returned to the ship, and weighed for Aboh, off which we anchored in the afternoon. I went on shore immediately in the same boat with Captain Taylor, Dr. Hutchinson, and Mr. Richards. We landed Aliheli, the Haussa interpreter, here. Aboh was found in the same state as Ossamare. Although the river had fallen four feet, our boat pulled within six yards of Aje's house, to which we had about five minutes' walk from the creek at our first landing, July 22. Large trading canoes were afloat opposite the houses in the cross streets ; and as the water falls, the mud and puddle is left to be waded through by the people as they pass to and fro in the town. We managed, partly by skipping or tiptoeing over the mud to get into Aje's house, but some of the gentlemen had to be carried on men's shoulders. Aje's house being built upon a mound above the level of the water, was compara-

tively dry; but the square was very damp, and
green algæ covered some parts of it. Aje received
us with much joy; and that we might enjoy our
interview, unmolested by the crowd in the open
but muddy inner square, he invited us into his
private chamber, which had two or three pigeon
holes as windows, to admit air and light. He
desired us to sit down either on the mat he had
spread for our accommodation, or, those who preferred it, on the chair and stool he brought in.
But this inner room was so dark that we could
scarcely see one another's faces, and very close from
so many sitting together, within so small a compass.
We therefore preferred the noise in the open square
to the smothering of the dark private closet; and
went out again. I asked for Simon Jonas, who
was then at Tshukuma's house, and he was immediately sent for. After Captain Taylor and Dr.
Hutchinson had done with trading business, I briefly
introduced the subject of the contemplated missionary establishment among them, but deferred
entering at length into particulars till I could see
him and his brother Tshukuma together. He said
he knew all about it, and that all would be right.
I then invited him on board to-morrow morning
with his brother Tshukuma, according to the request of Dr. Baikie. We left Aje, and went on
a visit to his younger brother Okoya, who, Simon
Jonas said, was very kind to him, and expressed
his wish many times to see me on my return from
the Tshadda. He was very glad to see me, and
entertained us with palm wine and kola nuts;

and I invited him with his brother on board to-
morrow. Leaving Okoya, we paid a visit to Tshukuma who was very glad to see me again, and
made anxious enquiries after the ship's crew. When
I told him that we had all returned as we went,
without losing a man, either by sickness or accident,
he grasped me by the hand with repeated greeting,
and said, "Your ship is a singular instance," and
that we were more fortunate than all the vessels
that ever visited this river. When I told him how
far we had been, and that I had visited Hamaruwa, and spoken with the Filani king upon the
subject of the white man's religion, and that he
consented to let his people be taught,—Tshukuma
was surprised, and looked upon me as if I had
been to the end of the world. He asked, Did you
see and speak with the king of the Filanis? I said,
yes; and that Dr. Baikie had visited and spoken
with him too, though it took us three days to go
to him from the water-side and back to the ship.
Tshukuma pointed to three little boys standing by,
and said, the Filanis sold all these. I told him
that he offered to present Dr. Baikie with two
slaves, but they were refused, and he was told it
was sinful to possess slaves. Tshukuma could say
no more, but listened to my brief relation of our
visit to the countries up the river with perfect
astonishment. Some traders had seen us at Rogan-
koto in September, and reported at Aboh that we
had gone to the black waters, the country occupied
by the Filanis, the disturbers of the world; hence their
fear and apprehension for our safety. I invited him

on board with Aje his brother, according to the
request of Dr. Baikie. We left Aliheli on shore,
and took Simon Jonas on board with us. Tshukuma requested that a boat should be sent for him
to-morrow, which request I promised to make to
Dr. Baikie.

November 1 : After breakfast, the gig was sent
for Tshukuma and Aje according to promise. The
former came in the gig, but Aje came in state in
his own large canoe, paddled by thirty pullaboys,
with about thirty others, including eight or ten of
their wives who accompanied their husbands on
board. Tshukuma was dressed in plain white Turkey trousers, and a white English shirt and jacket,
as when he visited the ship three months ago ; but
Aje appeared in superfine scarlet Turkey trousers,
and a scarlet serjeant's coat with a string of large
pipe corals thrown over the collar. Both had red
hats on their heads. Aje reminded me of his father,
whom he resembled much both in dress and gait,
and in his keenness as a trader.

After the usual salutations, Dr. Baikie had a
long talk with them, after which I introduced the
subject of resident Christian teachers. Tshukuma
and Aje had consulted together on the matter previous to our arrival, and said that they were quite
willing to receive them, but that the fault rested
with us, for we had deceived them before in raising
their expectation when their father was alive ; and
now they hesitated to believe till they see us fulfil
our promise. I then explained the cause of the
delay, but expressed my hope that it would not be

long before our purpose was effected; telling them that it was on that account I had left Simon Jonas with them, that they might have time to think sufficiently on the matter. They said, Simon Jonas could bear testimony to their willingness, but the rest remains with us.

During the three months Simon Jonas remained at Aboh, he was treated with a degree of kindness and respect, by Tshukuma and Aje, which quite exceeded our utmost expectations. He was taken ill two weeks after we left, and continued ill a week. He was then in Tshukuma's house; he says that the care and attention received from him, was like that of a father. He was sent for by different chiefs in the town, for conversation, and to ascertain whether what was said respecting our intention to form an establishment at Aboh, was likely to be carried out. He often spoke to them about their superstitious practices as being foolish, and one of them, that of chewing a stick to clean the teeth, and then spitting before their country fashion, to invoke a blessing upon those who desired their good, imprecating his anger upon those who desire their hurt, was given up by some upon his representing to them the folly of so doing. He found them teachable, inquisitive, and attentive to what was told them, and if proper attention were paid to them, much good might be done.

Simon Jonas moved about among them as a person of influence, from his superior knowledge, and travelled a day's journey inland to Oko-Ala. At this place he was asked by the chief, why we were going to remain at Aboh, and not with them also in Oko-Ala? Jonas could only tell him, that no place would be left unvisited in due time. He returned from Oko-Ala the third day fearing that the steamer might arrive in his absence. He then went to Asaba and Onitsha markets by water. These places are about the limit of the Aboh territory. He also visited Akra-Atani, Ossamare, Ogume, and Omu-Osai: in all which places he was well received. At Aboh, one little boy could say all the letters of the alphabet, others have learned some letters. Tshukuma had shown Simon Jonas a place near his own abode, where he thought a house might be built for us, if I thought it suitable on my return. He had examined the entire place according to my direction, and now left it to me to judge of the different localities for myself.

November 2: After breakfast I went on shore with Captain Taylor, and Dr. Hutchinson. Mr. Richards accompanied me, and we went first to Aje's house. While sitting in a private room, about 10 feet by 5, which received light through six pigeon-hole windows, as we were remarking about the length and breadth of the rooms, a petition came from two prisoners, through Simon Jonas, that we should intercede with Aje on their behalf. Being requested to mediate, I called the chiefs attention to the subject. I first proved the justice of rewarding the good, and punishing the evil; saying, that it was so in all parts of the world. After leaving the matter to work an impression upon his mind, I interceded for the prisoners, that they might be released for our sake. Aje was struck, he paused a little, spoke to one of his attendants, and then requested us to come to the square, where the prisoners had been bound, neck and feet, with chains, for the last twenty days. There he seated us, and requested me to repeat what I had said to him in his private chamber. This I did in the hearing of those present, and of the prisoners themselves. Aje replied, in the presence of his people, that we were true people, that he would not refuse any thing we wished him to do; that if he was about to execute a person, and we were to tell him to forbear, he would do so; that if he was about to sell a person, and we should forbid it, he would desist, and that he would act now according to our request. He then immediately ordered the two prisoners to be set at liberty. As I had landed purposely to go through the town, I took Simon Jonas with me, and left Captain Taylor and Dr. Hutchinson with the chief, to talk about trading. I visited Tshukuma, had some conversation with him, and told him that I was going to walk through the whole of Aboh. He said he apprehended some difficulty in doing so, on account of the mud and water in the cross streets, but I told him that I had come for the purpose and was determined to go through it. Tshukuma was very much in want of a chest to keep his clothes in. When Simon Jonas was here in 1841, he gave him one of his, and the chief now presented Jonas with a country cloth, for which he wanted a box in return; Simon could not spare the only one he had, and when I

came in, Tshukuma told me of Simon's refusal to
accept his present.   Simon then explained the matter,
and the chief pressed upon him the cloth or linen,
which I told him to accept.   I wrote Tshukuma's
want of a box in my note book, and requested him
to be patient till next year, when I hoped he would
receive one.   He offered to make me a present
of a ram, which I requested him to keep till next
year, please God, for the entertainment of my friends
who might come; and we took our leave.   I next
paid a visit to Isaba, an old man, whom I may call
the King's Counsellor.   He is the keeper of the
suits and other articles used when the king goes
through the ceremonial of being acknowledged as
the sovereign of the nation.   Since the death of
the late Obi Osai, no one has been elected king in his
stead, and Isaba has been acting as the president
of Aboh.   All important matters are therefore referred to him for decision, though Aje assumes the
air of royalty, on account of his wealth, influence,
and power; and being an active and intelligent man,
he is feared by the people.   Isaba was very glad to see
me, and asked whether Tshukuma had not mentioned
his name to me; as he had not done so, I informed
Isaba that Tshukuma had promised to tell all the
head chiefs what I had said to him, and observed
that I did not doubt but that he, Isaba, was the
principal person intended.   The thought that he
was not slighted pleased him; I then told Isaba
that I had heard of his great name, and came to
apprise him of our intention to send some Ibo
teachers to Aboh, to reside there and teach the

people God's book, and white man's fashion. He expressed his joy at the idea, and said that he had a female relation in Sierra Leone, whom he would be very glad to see at Aboh. This relative I afterwards understood to be the wife of J. Grant, one of the Ibo interpreters, who had visited Isaba the evening before. He entertained us with kola nuts. Leaving Isaba's house, I commenced my inspection of the town, from N.E. to S.W. it is fully a mile in length, and about 200 yards in breadth, lying parallel with the creek, with a wide opening along side the creek, the cross streets running nearly east and west. The greatest disadvantage to Aboh is the creeks formed up their streets at the rising of the river. The people themselves help much towards it, by digging clay in the streets, and in the front of their houses; and the holes admit water at every rise of the river. Thus what was before regular streets, are now nothing but so many small creeks through the town. Moreover, they widen and deepen the streets, that canoes may be brought nearer their houses at high water. From these causes, the state of the long and cross streets was such that I should have had greater facility in my inspection had we been a week earlier, for I could have gone over the whole in a canoe paddled from house to house, but the river having fallen four feet already, nothing but mud remained, except where the water was deep enough for a canoe; and I had to wade through the streets. The sites of the houses, and the huge cotton-trees are undermined by the encroaching stream, though they still maintain their hold. But

the fall of a tree would carry with it the ruin of
many houses, and risk the life of their inmates.
Other spots, sheltered by sacred groves and bushes,
are not suffered to be cleansed, but left untouched,
to be the receptacle of filth. This state of things
served to show the real height of Aboh above the
level of the water, before it was spoiled through the
foolishness of the people. The south-west end of
the town being but recently inhabited, has not yet
suffered so much as the north-east; but the same
plan of digging pits in the streets, and from the
water's edge, is followed there also. At this end of
the town, towards the entrance of the creek, within
a short distance of the vessel's anchorage, in the
main river, I have fixed upon a spot of land for a
contemplated Mission establishment, and given Aje
a strict charge not to suffer any of his people to
meddle with the place, or allow the near neighbours
to dig away the soil (which is in a great measure
sandy), that no water may encroach and spoil that
part also. Aje said, the land was his, and he would
take care of it for us. I have taken this step to
secure the spot at once, as being the best I could at
the time discover. It will be left to those who may
have to commence Missionary operations here, to use
their own discretion when upon the spot. But after
all that can be done, the place can only be occupied
by native teachers. I cannot recommend it for the
residence of European Missionaries, though they may
occasionally visit it from the upper and healthier
parts of the country.

Having proved the good-will of the chiefs and

people, the respect they have for their countrymen who have enjoyed greater advantages than themselves, their willingness to be taught, and their anxious expectation to see us fulfil the promise long made to their late king in this respect—I cannot but conclude my report of Aboh by saying, I assuredly gather that the Lord hath called the Church to preach the Gospel to them.

In the evening, we shifted from our anchorage, and dropped a mile below Aboh into the open stream.

November 3: Weighed early this morning, and anchored off Agberi, the first Oru village below the Aboh district. Here we purchased fuel, of which the people had a large quantity for their own use, as they keep fires almost always burning in their houses, to dry them, and counteract the damp which proves so injurious to the inhabitants of the Delta. There were two headmen in the village, one an old man, called Igbemà, and the other a much younger person, called Agbekun. The latter visited our ship when aground above Truro island on the 18th of July. Since that time Agbekun has been absent at Arò, the capital of a district of that name near Isuama, where the Tshuku, the great god of the Ibos, resides. Agbekun, being childless, went thither to inquire of the god. While there, he went through many ceremonies, and performed many sacrifices; and had just returned with a favourable answer from Tshuku, whom, however, he himself did not see, because all communication with him must be carried on through the priests. He brought back some representations of guardian gods from Tshuku, three of which he showed us as a proof that he had truly been in the place of Tshuku. This is always reported to be at a distance of about three months' journey, though Agbekun performed it and back, with the performance of all the ceremonies, within that period. This gave me the opportunity of speaking to him about the true God, to whom I endeavoured to turn his attention to look for blessings, both temporal and spiritual. He wanted to know how to pray to the Great God, whom he knew to be greater than Tshuku. I told him to do so, just as a little child would ask his father for what he is in need of. Agbekun was very shy in speaking much about the Tshuku of the Ibos, as a great mystery is connected even with the place of his residence. Since his return, he has been going through some ceremonies, and cannot be seen or spoken to much in public, till the time allotted to them has expired, which will be in about two days. In consequence of this, he did not attend market; but he was told, that as we were from white man's country, his ceremony could not be spoiled by his conversation with us. He replied, "There is no hatred in white man's country as in black man's country." I told him to look at me, a Yoruba by birth; Simon Jonas, an Ibo ; and Dr. Baikie, an Englishman; though of different nations, we live together as brethren, and so our God teaches all men to love one another. I expressed my hope that we should soon be able to teach them this love, which he was glad to hear. When comparing Oru and Brass, or Itebu words together, his attention was called off to settle some mistake made about the pur-

chase of wood outside. Dr. Baikie pointed out to
me an Arò man, Okori by name, a blacksmith, who
had lately come to Agberi with his son, with whom
we had some conversation. He told us the names of
some places of importance on the way to Arò, by the
Bonny river, above Aboh; he knew the town of Simon
Jonas, in Isuama, not far from Arò. At noon we
weighed from Agberi, and anchored at the lower end
of the branch explored by the Wilberforce, a mile or
two above Angiama.*

November 4: We dropped down to Angiama to
visit the chief, as well as to purchase some wood.
This place was completely swamped; how the people
could live there I really could not conceive. We
were seated in an unfinished house, when Ndawa, the
chief, made his appearance. He was the same person
who requested that the ship should stop and trade on
our ascent. Dr. Baikie gave him a present of some
red cloth as a kind of inducement to get his people
to sell wood, of which they had abundance, owned by
the women, piled up in large heaps under their store
houses. These houses are erected upon sticks about
four feet high from the ground, to avoid damp and
moisture, and separate from their group of dwellings,
to avoid fire, which may break out among them. In
a very short time, plenty of dry wood was bought
for scissors, needles, snuff-boxes, and brass ferret-bells,
with which they were exceedingly delighted. The
chief invited Dr. Baikie on shore to his house, and
presented him with a sheep, yams, and cocoa-nuts.
The Doctor impressed upon him the necessity of

* See Schön and Crowther's Journal, p. 38.

maintaining friendship with white men, that trade
might be carried on with him as well as with other
chiefs in the interior and on the river. He then gave
the chief a red serge cloak, which was very acceptable ; and he promised to see that no molestation
was offered to any boat or canoe belonging to us,
which may go up or down the river. It will be remembered that this was the place where Mr. Lander
was mortally wounded. Having completed our business at Angiama, we weighed about nine A.M., and were
once more in sight of the salt water at a quarter-past
two P.M., dropping anchor about an hour after—just
sixteen weeks, this very day, since leaving the spot.

Here again we have cause to raise our Ebenezer
to God, who has led us out, and brought us in, in
safety, both Europeans and Natives, without losing a
single person either from sickness or accident.

November 5, Sunday : We lay at anchor, and
preparations were made for crossing the bar on Monday. Mr. May, accompanied by Mr. Richards, left
the ship early in the morning on a visit to Brass
River, by the creek. They returned a little before
sunset, but brought no news of any importance, neither letter nor newspaper. I held Divine service at
half-past ten, and preached from Joshua xiv. 6 and 7.
All the officers on board manifested an earnest desire
to return thanks to the Lord, who has so mercifully
dealt with us during our voyage up the river.

November 6 : Steam was got up before daylight,
and as soon as we could see sufficiently, taking advantage of high water, by seven o'clock, the ' Pleiad,'
piloted by Mr. Richards, crossed the bar in smooth

water, as if she was sailing in Clarence Cove. Here are again additional mercies, for which we cannot be thankful enough. About noon, the schooner 'Mary,' Captain Robertson, from Bonny, hove in sight. We came up to her, when Mr. Robertson boarded us, and brought a newspaper as late as August 19. He also gave us some news about the coast, and said that the mail steamer 'Ethiope' had left only about two days before. It was cheering, after four months' absence in the river, without communication with our friends, to hear news again of the civilized world.

November 7: Fernando Po was in sight this morning; and about five P.M. we dropped anchor in Clarence Cove, having been boarded by Mr. Mackenzie a short time before. We soon landed, and were received by Governor Lynslager, Rev. Mr. Diboll, the Baptist Missionary, and all the native settlers, with heartfelt gratitude that we all have been spared to return from the river in good health and spirits.

May this singular instance of God's favour and protection drive us nearer to the throne of grace, to humble ourselves before our God, whose instruments we are, and who can continue or dispense with our services, as it seems good to His unerring wisdom.

SAMUEL CROWTHER.

APPENDIX.

APPENDIX I.

THE COUNTRIES ON THE BANKS OF THE NIGER AND BINUE.

Abbeokuta, Jan. 1855.

REV. AND DEAR SIR,

I could not complete my notices of the countries and languages on the banks of the Niger and Binue, in Central Africa, by the time I left the 'Bacchante,' which sailed for England last month, so I hope at this time to put you in possession of those notices, trusting they will be helpful in some respects in future researches in those countries.

You will be aware that the people we passed in our ascent are the Oru and Abọ in the Delta, the Igarra on the left of the Niger, the Kakanda at the Confluence of the Kowara and Tshadda, the Igbira, Bassa, Doma, Mitshi, and Djuku, otherwise called Apa, or Akpa, or Baibai, the language of Kororofa, and the Fulah on the Binue.

1. The Oru, or Ijo, or Udsọ of Koelle are identical with Brass, at the mouth of the Nun, on the coast, otherwise called Itẹbu or Nẹmpe, by their Ibo neighbours. This language is spoken to the extent of 100 miles from the mouth of the Nun, to the boundary of Abọ territory: how far inland towards Benin, on the right and towards the Ibo country, on the left of the Niger, is yet unknown.

2. The Abọ is a dialect of the Ibo language,

commencing from about the Benin branch of the Niger, and extending to Asaba (Onia market of Trotter). It comprises a district of about 50 or 60 miles along the banks of the Niger, and is very extensively spoken in its various dialects in the countries inland, on the left bank of the Niger, as far as we could ascertain, from the information we collected, to Cross River, on the back of Old Calabar ; the Calabar or Efik and Bonny trade with the Ibo in the interior,—Isoama seems to be the leading or popular dialect of this language ; all Ibo people who meet together in Sierra Leone, whether of the Abo, Elugu, Aro, or Abadja tribe, speak Isoama, and it has been recommended as the best to be used in the translations into the Ibo language : the Rev. J. F. Schön translated his vocabulary in this dialect. The Bonny or Okoloma, and New Calabar language is different from the Ibo, and from the fact that Bonny is principally peopled by Ibo slaves, and their continued intercourse with the Ibo of the interior, it may be inferred that in course of time, the Ibo language will gain advantage over the Bonny, which is very limited on the coast, when books are published in the Ibo language.

3. The next country after the Ibo, on the banks of the Niger is Igarra, the language of Igarra is the same as the Akpotto and is spoken from Adamugu to the Confluence of the Kowara and Tshadda, to the extent of 110 miles on the banks of the Niger. It is also extensively spoken inland on the left bank of the Niger, to the Mitshi country, on the left bank of the Binue—about the longitude of Ojogo. This

language appears to be a mixture of Yoruba and the original Akpọttọ ; its comparison with the Yoruba in the accompanying table will at once shew their relationship.

4. The Kakanda is the next country on the banks of the Niger, and the language is a dialect of Yoruba. This people have been so much driven about, that the limits of their country are very difficult to ascertain ; they inhabited the mountains on the right side of the Kowara and border on Nupe : at present they inhabit chiefly the left banks of the Niger, below the Confluence, since they were expelled from their mountain holds, by Dasaba, King of Nupe.

5. The next country after the Kakanda is Nupe, very much unsettled about the time of our visit. It has not therefore been explored.

6. From the Confluence on the right side of the Tshadda, is the Igbira country, called Koto by the Haussa, and Kotokori by the Yoruba ; since their country has been overrun by the Felatas, they have removed to the left side of the river, in the country of Akpọttọ. Their language is different from Igarra. There is also a tribe of this people called Igbira Hima, on the right side of the Niger between Idda and the Confluence.

7. The next country after Igbira, on the right side of the Tshadda is Bassa, whose language appears to be a distant dialect of the Nupe. Their country has also been overrun by the Felatas, and they were obliged to seek refuge in Akpọttọ land, after the example of their neighbours the Igbira.

8. The next country on the right side of the Tshadda, is Doma, also called Arago, a tribe of which is called Agatu, inhabiting Akpotto land on the left side of the Tshadda, to which they had been driven by the Felani. I shall annex a comparative table of the language, as it also appears to me to be of the Yoruba class, if not Yoruba in its origin.

9. The next country on the left side of the Tshadda, is the Mitshi, whose language is very little known and very peculiar to itself. The Mitshi country commences as it appears opposite Ojogo, and is mixed with the Akpotto and with Kororofa from which it is difficult to distinguish the boundaries. They are chiefly independent, but some portion of them pay tribute to Wukari, King of Kororofa.

10. The next country after the Mitshi, is extensive,—Kororofa having, Wukari for its capital, and the language spoken is Djuku, commonly called Akpa, but they call themselves Baibai. The language is spoken as far as Hamaruwa, now under the government of Mohamma, the Felani Sultan of that country.

11. The next language we met with on the Binue, is the Felani.

12. The most important of all is the Haussa, the commercial language of Central Africa.*

From the above enumeration of languages, it will be seen that twelve distinct translations will be necessary to diffuse Christianity right and left on the banks of the Niger and Tshadda, and into

* For the extent of each country on the banks of the river, see the Map at the commencement of the volume.

the interior as far as these languages are spoken ;
the same will be applicable in commercial intercourse with those nations : but there is a fact which
has not been sufficiently noticed, that is, the facility
which is given in communicating with these different
nations on the banks of the Kowara and Binue,
through the medium of the Haussa language, which
is extensively spoken by the different tribes, with
whom we had communication.

From Oru in the Delta, we already commenced
meeting with solitary opportunities of communicating
with the people, through Haussa slaves.   From
Abo we engaged an Haussa interpreter who was
very serviceable to us throughout the Expedition.
At Idda we found that the Haussa language was
becoming more generally spoken by the inhabitants.
Salutations in that language generally sounded in
our ears.   At Igbegbe near the Confluence, the
Haussa is one of the prevailing languages spoken
by the mixed population of that market town, and
it is the chief medium of communication in commercial transactions, though Igbira is the language
of the place.

At Yimaha in the Igbira country, at Oruko in the
Bassa country, at Doma, also among the hitherto unknown Mitshis, among the inhabitants of extensive Kororofa, and with the Filanis of Hamaruwa, the Haussa
language was the chief medium of communication,
both with the chiefs and the people whom we visited
during the late Expedition, and I was told that the
knowledge of Haussa will bring any one to Mecca.
From Igarra and upwards, though each language

must ultimately be learnt, and translations be made into it, yet it appears to me, that a good translation into the Haussa language, for general use for travelling Missionaries among the nations above mentioned, will not fail to be of an invaluable advantage; this language seems to me, destined by God to be the general medium of imparting the knowledge of Christianity, to a very great extent among the nations by whom it is spoken, when we take the Haussa themselves of Kano, Katshina, Zanfara, and other tribes speaking that language as their own, into consideration: all the Mahommedans understand and speak the Haussa language, and through it the Koran is explained and interpreted in their mosques throughout Yoruba. So that from Lagos, Badagry, and Porto Novo, and upwards to the Niger, where Mahommedans are found, the Haussa language is spoken by them. Now, if we glance on the map, it will be at once seen to what extent this language is spoken, and its general usefulness in every respect.

From this circumstance, I may suggest that the reduction of the Haussa language is of very great importance, especially if there is any probability of an annual visit to the Niger and Binue by steam-vessels, for the purpose of commerce; and even if no attempt can yet be made to commence Missionary operations about the Confluence of the Kowara and Tshadda, such translations will be of general use among whatever tribes the travellers go. Schön's Vocabulary needs to be revised and improved. I shall be ready to contribute what I have now in possession towards such improvement when required.

Here I am led to remark the usefulness of Koelle's Polyglotta Africana. The languages above enumerated, except the Doma and Mitshi,* were found among his specimens; and in those cases no time was wasted in attempting to correct him, for these reasons—1st. It was sufficient to know he has got specimens of the language, constituting a good guide, and time would be lost in going over the same ground again. 2nd. The correction attempted might be useless, because one tribe may pronounce the same thing one way, and another another way, by changing letters; for instance—

English.	Oru.	Brass or Itebu.
Water	Megi	Migi
Fire	Feni	Fendi

among the Oru, and Brass, or Nempe. But *additional* words or phrases contributed to his few specimens, would tend to make the language better known. 3rd. The time was too short to do it properly.

In looking over Mr. Koelle's collections, I could not help regretting that he has sometimes spent enormous labour in repeating, as many as twelve specimens, as under the head of Aku, what are merely variations in dialect and not of language; the seeming difference being no greater than that each tribe would pronounce the same word according to his peculiar tone or accent. The word would be commonly understood, it being no other language, —though sometimes different words are given; but

* See note, p. 234.

these are not many. I could increase the dialects
of the Yoruba tongue to twice that number, and
yet two translations are not necessary among them.
The same remark is applicable to Mr. Koelle's
two specimens, under Haussa of Kano, and Katshina; and his five specimens of Ibo, under Isoama,—the change of *r* for *l*, or for *n*, *s* for *sh*, is
very common, and constitutes in many cases the
chief difference of a tribe. The people from different
tribes meeting to transact their usual business do not
take much notice of their difference in this respect,
so long as they can understand one another; therefore, their being written as specimens, beyond enumeration of the tribes under a certain head, seems to
be unnecessary. But the work is a valuable pro-
duction, and of great utility to a great distance in
Western Central Africa.*

There are three places which go by the name
of Ado about this part of the country. One is south
of Otta, twenty miles north of Badagry; one is
not far from Isehin, in the Yoruba country; one is
between Benin and Abo, inland, on the right side of
the Niger, opposite Adamugu. This last Ado appears
to be not far from Ijesa country, near Ife, and among
the following group of tribes of Yoruba dialects ; viz.:
Ijamò,`Efon, Ondo, Idoko, Igbomna, Ife, Ijesa, Ado.
This last is the Ado mistaken for the one near Badagry by Mr. Koelle, consequently the position of his
Ijesa in that place is wrong ; the situation of Ijesa
near Ife, north of Ijebu, will be more correct.

* The Map accompanying this volume will correct, in some
measure, Mr. Koelle's positions of those countries visited by
the Expedition.

Isoama, in the Ibo country, is on the left side of the Niger, north of Aro, and not on the right, as Mr. Koelle was informed, but an accurate knowledge of these places can only be obtained by further researches.

I cannot bring these notices to a close without again pressing the necessity of immediate steps being taken, when another Expedition ascends the river, to locate some persons of the Ibo nation in the town of Abo, and, if possible, also some Christian teachers at the Confluence of the Kowara and Tshadda; the latter is a nucleus of trade between the natives of the interior, and the situation most important. When two or three yearly visits in succession are made by steam-ships, there will be mutual understanding between England and the inhabitants of the Delta, the river will be opened for our boats and canoes, as the Ogun is at present with us in Abbeokuta. It is my belief, and I do not express it from a momentary excitement, that the Niger Mission may yearly be visited by prudent and experienced Missionaries from the Yoruba country. It only requires that seasonable opportunity be seized to open the way, and keep a chain of communication between this and the Niger, so that in case there is no opportunity of visiting it by steam from the sea, the Mission will not be neglected, when it can be visited by the land route.

APPENDIX II.

1. COMPARISON OF LANGUAGES.

English.	Igarra.*	Yoruba.
A large thing	Nhun yi nanna	Ohun yi nila
A small thing	Nhun yi yan	Ohun yi kere
White book	Takarda funfun	Takarda funfun
Black book	Takarda dudu	Takarda dudu
Black man	Enia dudu	Enia dudu
This thing is good	Nhun yi yọn	Ohun yi dara
A bad person	{ Enni ibi (evil of Yoruba)	} Enia or Enni buburu
Old cloth	Igbo ìpo	Aṣo gbigbo
Old man	Onia anagbo	Enia arugbo
A young man	Onia kolobia	Ommọ kọnri enia
I am sick	Ọgá mu mi	Arọn mu mi
I am well	Ọgá mi tan	Arọn mi tan
It is hot	{ Emi jo (jo, to burn, is used)	} Omi gbona
I am cold	Afun apa mi	Otutu mu mi
The cloth is wet	'Ipo yi tsomi	Aṣo yi tutu
My cloth is dry	'Ipo mi gbẹ	Aṣo mi gbẹ
This person is greedy	Enni pari	Enni yi lawọn
A stupid person	Enni dàda	Enia gigò
A rich person	Enni etṣe nuhun	{ Enni ti o ṣolohun, or olowo
A poor person	Enni ale	Enni oluponju
A straight stick	{ Ori ki bòro, Nle yanja	} Iggi titọ
A crooked stick	Ori ki gò	Iggi wiwọ

* See my remarks on this language in my Journal of the Expedition, 1854, p. 355.

English.	Igarra.	Yoruba.
Governor of a province, entitled King	Onu	Olu
Medicine	Ogun	Ogun
Face	Eju	Iwaju
Nose	Imọ	Imọ
Ear	Eti	Eti
Mouth	Alu	Ẹnnu
Tooth	Eyin	Eyin or Ehin

But other words are entirely distinct, as in

Blood	Ebia	Ejẹ
Small Pox	Oyasuma	Ṣanpanna, &c.

English.	Doma.	Yoruba.
Ear-ring	Oruka	Oruka eti
Fire	Olá, from Yoruba, lá, to lick	Ina
Axe	Akeke	Akeke or Ãke
Sun	Enọ	Orùn
Dry season	Ọnọ	Ẹrùn
Thread, cotton	Owu	Owu
Rope	Ongua	Okun
Tree	Okpa, Opa, Yoruba word for a stick	Iggi
Walking-stick	Okute, Okaje, from Yoruba, Ekutẹ, post	Ọpa
Yam	Iṣi	Iṣu

English.	Doma.	Yoruba.
Onion	Alibọsa	Alubọsa
Horse	Ọyan, from Yoruba *Yan*, to neigh, to gape	Ẹṣin
Milk	Amẹ	Omu
Egg	Ayi	Ẹyin
Musquito	Emia, from Yoruba *Eminrin*, sandfly	
House	Ole	Ille
Leopard	Ẹjẹ, from Yoruba *Jẹ*, to eat	Ekùn
Chameleon	Oyan yan, from Yoruba, *Yan*, to walk leisurely	Agẹmọ
Frog	Okiritu, from Yoruba, *Kirifo*, a leaping, roving about	Opọllọ
White man	Oyibo	Oyibo
Young	Opẹpẹ	Opepe, a young person

---

2. PERSONAL PRONOUNS.

I	Ami, Na, Ni, Nga, M. N.	Emi, Mo, Mọ, Ng
Thou	Awọ, O	Iwọ, Ọ
He, she, it	Anu	On
We	Awa	Awa
You	Ãni	Ẹnyin
They	Alọ	Awọn

English.	Doma.	Yoruba.
We three sit down	Awa setta awa ayaje	Awa metta awa joko
You three sit down	Ani setta ani ayaje	Enyin metta enyin joko
They three sit down	Alo setta alo ayaje	Awon metta awon joko

---

3. REFLECTIVE PRONOUNS.

I myself	Amu amu obohin	Emiti karami
Thou thyself	Oyi iwo ne	Iwoti karare
He himself	Ase ni abohinu	Onti karare
We ourselves	Awo bokiwo	Awati karawa
They themselves	Alo bokigalo	Awonti karawon

Some words are borrowed from the Haussa.

English.	Doma.	Haussa.
Book	Takarda	Takarda
Ink	{ Orubutu, from Ru-butu, to write }	Tadawà
Rice	Sinkafa	Sinkafa
Ram	Rago	Rago
Lead	Aderema	Darima
Chain for neck	Asirika	Saraká
Drum	Okanga	Ganga

From the above comparison, it will be seen that the Doma appears to be a kindred language to the Yoruba, both from the formative prefix, construction of sentences, and by a careful trace of many of its words, which seem to have Yoruba roots and ideas for its origin: when the language is properly reduced, it will not unlikely be found to partake of Yoruba, and other neighbouring languages, with which it has become mixed in course of time, like that of the Igarra and Akpọttọ.

---

4. COMPARISON OF THE LANGUAGES OF THE DELTA.

English.	Oru or Ijọ.	Brass, Itẹbu or Nempe.	Bonny.
Water	Megi	Migi	Mingi
Fire	Fini	Fendi	Fene
Firewood	Fendia	Fingia	
Mat	Ute	Ute	Bile
House	Wale	Wale	Wari
Idol	Owu	Owu	Juju
God	Orisa	Orisa	Tamọnọ*

---

5. TERMINOLOGY FROM KING PEPPEL.

Bonny is called Okoloma by themselves,
　　　　　"　　　　Okoloba, Obani, or Ibani, by the Ibos.
　　　　　"　　　　Osiminiku by Abọ tribe of Ibo.
New Calabar is called Bom by the Ibo.

King Peppel said that Bonny was chiefly peopled by Ibo slaves, though they speak the Okoloma or Bonny language, which is also the language of New Calabar.

I remain, Rev. and Dear Sir,
Your obedient humble servant,
SAMUEL CROWTHER.

---

* This name, Peppel king of Bonny, told me is applicable to the true God, others more to country fashion.

6. TRANSLATIONS.

English.	Doma or Arago.	Mitshi.
One	Oye	Mọm
Two	Onpa	Hari
Three	Metta	Tara
Four	Mẹnni	Yin
Five	Meho	Tan
Six	Mihiri	Karmọn
Seven	Mohapa	Karhari
Eight	Mohata	Kartar
Nine	Mohani	Karyin
Ten	Iguo	Puẹ
Eleven	Iguo-roye	Puẹ karmọn
Twelve	Iguo-epà	Puẹ karhari
Thirteen	Iguo-ẹtta	Puẹ kartari
Fourteen	Iguo-ẹnni	Puẹ karyin
Fifteen	Iguo-eho	Puẹ kartan
Sixteen	Iguo-ihiri	Puẹ tartan
Seventeen	Iguo-apapa	Puẹ tankartan
Eighteen	Iguo-ahatan	Puẹ yinyin
Nineteen	Iguo-ahanni	Puẹ kartarkaryin
Twenty	Iniye-gasẹ	Kundu
Man	Osẹ	Numgusọ
Woman	Gboyin-ole	Kuasa
Boy		Wána
Girl		Guana
Father	Ada	
Mother	Enim	

* The Haussa being the medium of collection, *sh* has been retained to avoid two different modes of spelling.

English.	Doma or Arago.	Mitshi.
Grandfather	Osumoka	
Grandmother	Obohun	
Son	Oyimẹmẹ	
Daughter		
Elder Brother	Osum	
Younger Brother	Okinahin	
Elder Sister	Onumẹ	
Younger Sister	Okinahin	
Friend	`Ọya	Kará
Stranger	`Ọga	Worobanya
King	Ọssẹ	
Male Slave	Ofiẹ neyunro	
Female Slave	Ofiẹ niyan	
Doctor	Oboshi	
Medicine	Eshi	
Head	Eyin	Ntshowo
Hair	Eyin-ehù	Itshe
Face	Ogú	Ishigi
Forehead	Ogoyanma	Itshuru
Nose	Ewun	Shami
Eye	Iyepù	Eshie
Ear	Apaha	Ato
Mouth	Okonu	Ijua
Tooth	Ahunnu	Ayin
Tongue	Ẹnnẹ	Nọmburo
Throat	Ario-ogoyin	
Gullet		
Neck	`Okọ	
Shoulder	Atshọbọ	
Arm	Abọ	
Arm, between shoulder and elbow	} Igbọbo	

English.	Doma or Arago.	Mitshi.
Arm, between elbow and wrist	Mugabǫ	
Leg	Ikpo	
Outer hand, or hand	Abǫn	
Inner hand	Akpugabǫ	
Foot, or instep of the foot	Ikpo	
Foot sole	Ipugikpo	
Finger	Abǫ	
Toe	Okubikpo	
Elbow	Okekebǫbǫ	
Rib	Akoro	
Chest	Otu	
Female breast	Ame	
Belly	Ipu	
Navel	Ondo	
Thigh	Atǫku	
Knee	Okukù	
Heel	Ikpokitipi	
Nail of finger or toe	Ekugabǫ	
Skin	Okpakipie	
Bone	Kpoku	
Vein		
Blood	Oyi	
Itch	Ekkę	
Small Pox	Eleyanku	
Hat	Akata	
Cap	Otingira	
Shoe	Ǫkpa	
Shirt	Togbǫ	
Trousers	Owirikí	

English.	Doma or Arago.	Mitshi.
Waistcloth	Akiri, Zanua	Kondo
Town (village)	Oja, Oja yan ku	
Market	Izhi	Kazua, kasuạ
House	Olẹ	Yobọ
Door	Ozọgọ-ikole	
Doorway	Komiko ikoda	
Bed	Agodo	
Mat	Ozura	
Knife	Ẽwa	Thọ
Spoon	Ebu	
Ear-ring	Oriká	{ Hima (Iron ring to draw the bow)
Armlet, Bracelet	ͺOje	Kerifi
Pot	Ẽyi	Tiagẹ
Calabash, (large)	Obatu	Kapu
Calabash, (small)	Ogo	
Gun	Egbi	Burka
Powder	Ow	
Sword	Ewakpa	Ishomo
Spear	Okpa	Iwanga
Bow	Oyi	Ada
Arrow	Ota	Bana
Quiver	Ashangba	Gbanda
War	Efú	Tiaba
God	Oso	Wòndo
Devil	Eshí	
Idol	Ẹshí	
Greegree	Orio	
Sacrifice	Yobiriki nke	
Heaven (sky)	Oso	
Hell		

English.	Doma, or Arago.	Mitshi.
Fire	Olá	Wusu
Water	Eyìn	Ngoromi
Soup	Ibobo	
Meat (often animal)	Ẹbẹ	
Salt	Omua	
Gold	Ozanaria	
Iron	Oje, nofi	Akara
Stone	Ẹgọ	
Hoe	Fnu	
Axe	Akeke	
Book	Takarda	
Ink	Orubutu	
Sun	Enọ	
Moon (full)	Oya	
New Moon	Oya fufẹ	
Day	Enọ	
Night	Otu	
Dry season	Onọ	
Rainy season	Ọgua	
Rain	Oso, or uso	
Dew	Omẹ	
Coal	Ubì	
Smoke	Iwọla	
Soap	Ukọ̀	
Sand	Ojẹ	
Canoe	Owu,	Igbanda
Ship	Owugeibo	
Bench, chair	Ọkka	
Needle	Oyina	
Thread	Owu	

English.	Doma.	Mitshi.
Rope	Ongua	
Chain, fetters for the feet and neck	Ashirika, for the hand; Eye-otikpo, for the feet	
Drum	Okanga	
Tree	Okpa	
Fire-wood	Efu-kola	
Walking-stick	Okute-okaje	
Leaf	Epu	
Root	Egba ko kposhi	
Palm-tree	{ Ikpari, Ikposhi-kikpari }	Wure
Palm-oil	Anonowá	
Guinea-corn, with head like a maize	Iye	
Kuskus, bearing a head like oats	`Igu	
Cotton	Owu	
Cotton plant (a shrub)	Ikposhi-gowu	
Cotton tree	Ugú nigbije	
Cam wood	Oshigewo	
Rice (uncooked and cooked)	Shinkufa	
Yam	Ishi	Iyogo
Cassada	Okposhi	
Ground nut	Obonu	
Pepper	Akpoko	

English.	Doma.	Mitshi.
Onion	Alibọsa	
Maize	Ibakpa	
Beans	Eze	
Farm	Ehọ	
Forest	Okpá	
Horse	`Ọyan	
Mare	Oyan-leyan	
Cow	Enna	
Bull	Ẹnna-neyinro	
Milk (fresh and sour)	Amẹ	
Butter (fresh and melted)	Anangoyi	
Sheep, ewe	Adọgbọ	
Ram	Rago, tukpo	Lumu, or Numu Yimgọ
Goat	Ikpowu	Keme kusa
Buck		
Cat	Bantshakù	
Rat	Igú	
Pig	Orushu	
Bat	Ariga	
Pigeon	Mandegu	
Parrot	Okò	
Fowl (hen)	Ogu, ugu	
Cock	Obugu	
Egg	Ayi-ogu	
Bird	Igbanọ	
Fish	Ebẹ	
Serpent	Eguwa	
Scorpion	Ẹnna	

English.	*Doma.*	*Mitshi.*
Musquito	Emia	
Butterfly		
Spider		
Wasp		
Bee	Eho-ayikeho	
Honey	Eho	
Lion	`Idu	
Leopard	Eje	
Elephant	Adagba	
Ivory	Ahunnu	Shie, ivory ring
Alligator	Ikù	
Monkey	`Eka	
Chameleon	Oyanyan	
Lizard (common)	Apùwa	
Lizard (large red-headed)	Oyinkpaku	
Toad		
Frog	Akirifù	
Dog	Iwo	
Great, large	Yanko, yanku	
Little, small	Leke	
White	Onehe	
Black	Nobi	
White man	Oyinehe, oyibo	
Black man (negro)	(se-nobi	
Good	Oshi, ososhi	
Bad	Olabi	
Old (of things and persons)	Osenke	

English.	Doma.	Mitshi.
New (Young)	Opepẹ	
Sick	Agbẹre	
Well	Eshi	
Hot	Akola	
Cold	Soshia	
Wet	Ngeyin	
Dry	Oyinmọwẹ	
Greedy		
Stupid		
Rich		
Poor		
Straight	Onẹta	
Crooked (bent)	Ntọkọka	
I go	Agahún	
I come	Mu ọ wẹ	
I run	Na yin yàn	
I stop	Yinyan, ngan ikoyajẹ	
I sit down	Nga iyàjẹ	
I lie down	Ngbotá ngbọrẹ	
I breathe	Na showu	
I cough	Na kọkọ	
I sneeze	Na tashushu	
I snore	Na aholá	
I laugh	Na ayeyẹ	
I weep	Ami shiku	
I kneel	Nga kwajè	
I dream	Nẹnna	
I sleep	Agbolá	
I die	Oge ku	
I fall	Ngo nu	
I rise	Ni só	

English.	Doma.	Mitshi.
I speak	Ma ke lá	
I hear	Mpó	
I beg	Giam	
I bathe *or* wash myself	Nguyẹ	
I see	Mmá	
I take	Na ibise	
I buy	Nga rosa, ni ma ni	
I sell	Ni ira	
I love thee	Na doka họ	
I give thee	Ni zo họ	
I eat yam	Na ri ishi	
I drink water	Na goyin	
I cook meat	Ẹbe isọla	
I kill a fowl	Na mọ ogu	
I cut a tree	Nga she kposhi	
I flog a child	Na go ize	
I catch a fish	Nga ngbẹbẹ	
I break a stick	Lefi ki ngbo	
I call a slave	Na yi ogu ofiẹ	
I cover a pot	Na le yi isọla	
I sew a shirt or cloth	Na gọza ; Na ga kiri	
I pray to God (beg God)	Na bu Oso	
I play	Nga shiga	
I do not play	Nshiga nu, Onọ ga-shiga	
I dance	Nga gige	
I do not dance	Ngige nu	
Yesterday	Ẹnnẹ	

English.	Doma.	Mitshi.
To-day	Nkeni	
To-morrow	Oki	
Cowry	Ekuri	
Bowl	Okpara	
Lead	Aderema	
Brass	Oje	
Stars	Eyinyin-Owo	
Bead	Eke	
Shea-butter	Anaza	
Iron hoe, metal currency	Akika	Ibia
Red	Bèretete	Dodo (red cloth)
Bowl of a pipe	Tukunia	
Pipe	Turi	Etshu
Brass ring	Miki	
Flint		Pueni
Paddle		Nnaha
Post		Ikono
Canoe men	Osene powu	
Farmer	Adakeho, Ngbeho	
Fishermen	Nebe or Lebekue	
Trade	Ola	
Trader	Olola	
Judge	Ose she ba apotta	
Poison for arrow	Efa	
Antidote to poisoned arrow	Atekpa	
Hunter	Ose ne toite	
My father	Adam	

English.	*Doma.*
My mother	Oyam
My grandfather	Onkuọm
My grandmother	Amoyam
My stranger	Ozọga
My wife	Otshim
Black shoe	Okpa lobi, Takalmi nobi
Good morning	Ogà
I hope you rise well ?	{ Gbeshi nĩ, *or* Gbe shi gege nĩ ?
Do you hear ?	Opo nĩ ?
I hear	Mpo we
Leave it	Shabatá
A woman spins cotton	{ Oya jowu, *or* Gboyin ole jowu
Cock crows	Ogu tọnu
Egg breaks	Ayigu guitshia
Bird flies	Igbanọ yinso
Fish swims	Ebẹ tige iyọwọn
Snake bites	Ego (Eguwa) fọhunnu
Honey is sweet	Ẹhọ lọyan
Bee stings	Ẹhọ isum
Lion roars	`Idu shiku
Ivory is heavy	Ahìn gaba gbenu
Monkey skips	`Ẹka shobi
Dog barks	Ewo (Iwo) wonu
Sheep bleats	Adọgbọ degbà
Goat runs	Ipowu Oyinyọn
Pig squeaks	Orushu degbama
Rat burrows	Iyu yọ le

English.	*Doma.*
Alligator bites	Iku fosahunnu, *or* fahunnu
I buy an ivory	Nahin gaba ni la
A large cloth	Ekpa yankó
A small cloth	Ekpa leke
White paper	Takarda onehe
Old house	Oda osoneke
New house	Ole pepe
Hot water	Iyonlá, akola
Cold water	Eyin shoshia
Small cloth is wet	Akiri ngeyin
Large cloth is wet	Okpa ngeyin
Small cloth is dry	Akiri oyimowe
A straight stick	Kposhi oneta
A crooked stick	Kposhi ntokoka
This slave	Ofiè ni
You call me	Ami yo gurà
I call a boy	Oyi keke
A boy calls me	Oya ku yo igú
A red cap	Tingira nowa (yoyo)
A very high tree	Kposhi nyanka goga, Kposhi owiripo goga
I fall badly	Ngonu gburo
Very much	Agoga, agogagoga
The tree is very large	Kposhi o jaku goga
The glass is very dazzling	Ozomibe o mbe wàyawaya
This paper is very white	Takarda osehe gbogbo
This gun is very black	Bindiga o lobi wiri
The bird flies very high	Igbana o gizo gbogbo

English.	Doma.
The water is very full	Eyin lopajè gua yànyan
The wind blows very strong to-day	Ohu ta gogagoga nkeni
The night is very dark	Otu nkeni èbe dobugo gagoga
I eat in a bowl	Nlone ebe okpara
I cut with a knife	Lokoshe ti kewà
I drink water	Ngoyin
I am thirsty	Egin aw om
I myself	Amu-amu obohin
Thou myself	Oyi íwo nẽ
He himself	Ase ni abohinnu
We ourselves	Awo bo kiwo
You yourselves	
They themselves	Alo bo kigalo
Who ?	Onò koni ?
Whose ?	Ono kò gbo da ni ?
Which ?	Onò ko anú ?
What ?	Wu ka la ni ?
This ?	Onẽ ?
That ?	Olam nẽ ?
What are you thinking of ?	Ozhi ni oyi ne nè ?

7. PERSONAL PRONOUNS.

English.	*Doma.*
	Singular.
1. I	1. Ami, Na, Ni, Nga, contracted into M. N.
2. Thou	2. Awọ, o
3. He, she, it	3. Anu
	Plural.
1. We	1. Awa
2. You	2. Ani
3. They	3. Alọ
	Singular.
1. I eat	1. Ami ale
2. Thou eatest	2. Awọ ale
3. He eats	3. Anu ale
	Plural.
1. We eat	1. Awa ale
2. You eat	2. Ãni ale
3. They eat	3. Alọ ale

We three sit down	Awa setta awa ayajẹ
You three sit down	Ani setta ani ayajẹ
They three set down	Alọ setta alọ ayajẹ

8. COMPARISONS OF ORU AND BRASS, OR ITEBU.

English.	*Oru.*	*Brass or Itebu.*
Water	Megi	Migi
Fire	Feni	Fendi
Firewood	Fendia	Fingia
Mat	Ute	Ute
God	Orisha	Orisha

9. NOMENCLATURE OR TERMINOLOGY.

Eyọ or Yoruba is called Aku in Sierra Leone from salutation.

,,	,,	,,	Ayaji	by the	Nupe
,,	,,	,,	Yariba	,,	Haussa
,,	,,	,,	Anagonu or Inago	,,	Popọ
,,	,,	,,	Ayọnu	by the	Dahomey
Nupe	is called		Tapa or Takpa by the		Yoruba
Popọ	,,		Egùn	by the	,,
Dahomey	,,		Dada	,,	,,
Igbira and neighbouring countries is called			Kotokori	,,	,,
,,	,,		Koto	,,	Haussa
Kakanda	,,		Bunu	,,	,,
,,	,,		Shabẹ	,,	Igarras
Pulo	,,		Filani or Fulani	,,	Haussa & Yoruba
,,	,,		Felata	by the	Bornu
,,	,,		Angoyi	,,	Igbira
Doma, call themselves			Arɛgo		
Djukù or Baibai of Kororofa is called			Apa or Akpa by the		Igarra
Djuku & Mitshi are called			Akpa or Apa	,,	Ibo
Zhibu or Filani, slaves there are called			Katshara	,,	Djuku
Gandiko	,,		Gannako	,,	,,
Muri or Hamaruwa	,,		Kundi	,,	,,
Oru	,,		Ijọ or Ojọ	,,	Brass
Abọ or Aboh	,,		Oru	,,	Bonny
Bonny, properly Obani	,,		Okolobà	,,	Ibo
Brass, properly Nempe	,,		Itẹbu	,,	,,
Calabar, properly Efik	,,		Kalaban	,,	,,

Shekiri are called Iwinì by the Ibo.
Ado   „   Ido or Idu „   „
Abọ, Ibo or Igbo „   Opu   „ Igarra and all the
countries up the river.
Haussa is called Abakpa by the Igbira, Doma, Kororofa,
and other countries up the river.

---

10. *The Time of the Day.*

English.	*Haussa.*	*Pulo.*	*Yoruba.*
Cock-crowing	Asuba	⎱ Fajiri	⎰ Afemojumọ
Morning	Dasafe	⎰	⎱ Kùtukutu
About 8. A.M.	Anthin	Luha, Woluha	Owurò
„ 12. A.M.	Rana sakka	Najetshaka	Ossangangan
„ 2. P.M.	Azahar	Zura	Ayila
„ 4. P.M.	La Aser	Alazara	Asalẹ
Sunset	Almurù	Magaribà	Orunwọ
About 8. P.M.	Lisha	Eshaì	Allẹ

APPENDIX III.

1. *Route to Yola from Hamaruwa.*

Hamaruwa	6. Gangume	12. Dardio
1. Zhirù	7. Zongo ndoka	13. Hamedu, La-
2. Erima	8. Kogi mbaba	wal's brother
3. Zongo nkawo	9. Zhan garigari	14. Yola
4. Akam	10. Kwantshà	
5. Zongo nkangi	11. Laro	

The first five stages belong to Hamaruwa territory.

The remaining nine belong to Adamawa. This route of 14 days' journey is made round the Fumbina mountains by traders from Bantshi, Kano, and Katshina from the Haussa country, who trade in slaves and ivory, the road being safe under the government of the Filanis.

2. *Route to Yola by the course of the Binue.*

Hamaruwa	4. Tahiri subject to Lawal.
1. Wurobeli	5. Wuro Alahaji, only a short distance
2. Gowoi	to Yola
3. Zena.	

3. Zena. The Zenas are independent, and hostile to the Filanis: travellers who venture by this route must pass Zena in the night to avoid the attack of the pagans by day. Wurobeli and Gowoi are subject to Hamaruwa.

From Gandiko to Yola 15 days' journey

     ,,   ,,   ,, Wukari about 7 hours

    ,, Zhibu   ,,   ,,   ,, 1 day's journey, Zar market is in midway.

   ,, Anyishi ,,   ,,   ,, 3 days' journey
halting places, Akuana, Arufu, Afiayi.

   ,, Anyishi to Keana in Doma 1½ day, halting-place
Magede.

From Kwata on the left of the Binue to Wukari 2 days.

„ Zhibu to Gomkoi on the left of the Binue, 5 days.

„ „ Nyindo „ „ 5 days.

The Filanis were about to attack this place this dry season, one of them applied to me for a charm to enable him to catch slaves at Nyindo.

The following places were given, as being between Zhibu and the Confluence of the Binue and Faro or Paro, Zhibu, Belal, Djandurode, Kafe (chief Erima), Hama or Hamaruwa, Bàtshama, Bula, Dampsa, Garin, Tambul, Kenmi, Adamawa, Bunda at the Confluence of Binue and Paro or Faro.

---

3. *Route to Doma by Ojogo on the right of the Binue.*

Ojogo, Tunga, (a small village), Keana (large town), Kunduku, and Kalashi, (both small), Giza (large), Kireyi (small), Kodoroko (large), Kowara (small), Doma (large).

---

4. *Route from Rabba or Lade to Abbeokuta.*

Rabba, Gulufu, Saraji, Budo Alla Sariki.   } Oke-ʼOyi,
Lade, Lafiaji, Sambufu, Budo Alla Sariki. }
Ilori, Aimayò, Ojoku, Inisà, ʻIkiron, Osogbo, Edde of Timi, Iwo-ʼIsalle, Ijèhanna, ʻIbadan Ilugun, Oke Zoko, Abbeokuta.

Though Mahamma, the Yoruba traveller who is at present residing at the Confluence of the Kowara and Tshadda, in pursuit of his charm making trade, has made eighteen easy days' journey of this route, he said it could be accomplished in twelve days' hard push, if no hinderance took place on the way.

5. *Names of the Kowara and Tshadda.*

The Kowara is called Fari nrua (the white water) in general.

  ,,   ,, Oya by the Yoruba.

The Tshadda ,, Baiki nruwa (the black water) in ge-
          neral.

  ,,   ,, Nihu or Lihu by the Igbira.

  ,,   ,, Nu   ,, Djuku.

  ,,   ,, Binue   ,, Djuku and Filani.

The Niger ,, Osimirin by the Abo and the people
          of the Delta.

---

6. *States governed by the Filanis, according to Ibrahim, our guide at Hamaruwa.*

States.	Names of Governor.
1. Bagarmi	Sariki Bagarmi.
2. Adamawa	Lawal (Loèl of Dr. B.)
3. Hamaruwa	Mohamma.
4. Gòmbe	Koiranga.
5. Bornu	Sumanu.
6. Shira	Abduramanì.
7. Katagu	Dankaowà.
8. Marma	Mahamma.
9. Hadeji	Bohari.
10. Awoyò	Sambò.
11. Kano	Sumanu.
12. Kasawurai	Dembo.
13. Dawura	Zuheirù.
14. Katshina	Mohamma Bello.
15. Zanfara	Mamudu.

16. Gobiri	Ali.
17. Bautshi	Ibrahima.
18. Zozo (Zegzeg)	Sidì.
19. Dawudù	Badja.
20. Nufe, or Nupe	Dasaba.
21. Ilọrin	Abdusalami.
22. Yawuri	Sariki n Yawuri.
23. Kabì.	Sariki n Kabì.

Sokoto, the seat of government, and Alihù Sariki n Musulmin, or the sovereign of the faithful. Of these states, some are very extensive, and others small. Among the extensive states may be classed Adamawa, as far, according to Ibrahima, as to Igarra, and he believes that the Atta pays tribute to Lawal of Yola, through some intermediate channel. The state of Hamaruwa comprises all the countries on the banks of the Binue from Bautshi, including a part of Kororofa, of which Wukari is the capital, which however, pays tribute to Bautshi.

SAMUEL CROWTHER.

NOTE BY DR. WILLIAM BLEEK.

(To page 205.)

It is a mistake of Mr. Samuel Crowther's that his Mitshi Vocabulary gives us a totally unknown language. At the first look upon Kölle's Polyglotta Africana, I saw that here the Tíwi (XII. E. 19) shows only very slight dialectical differences. And in Kölle's Introductory Remarks, he says :—Tíwi, called Mîdṣi, or Mbídṣi, by the Kurórōfas and Haussas, and Gbâlon by the Agâyas, who speak the same language as the Tíwis. Herewith agrees Crowther's notice that the Djuku and Mitshi are called Akpa or Apa by the Ibu. Likewise indeed the Djukù, or Barbai of Kororofa, .are called Apa or Akpa by the Igbarra. Kölle's work is indeed an immense store of African knowledge, and its use would be still greater, if good indices were added of all the names of Languages, Nations, Countries, and places to be met with in his Introductory Remarks.

Still Mr. Crowther's Vocabularies are most important enlargements ; as Vocabularies, &c., made on the spot, are always preferable to such as are taken from individuals in places distant from their homes.